THE
FUTURE
OF AGING

AUTHORS

Mary Lou Ackerman
Taylor Dennis
Paul Holyoke, PhD
Zayna Khayat, PhD
Allyson Kinsley
Erik Landriault
Cameron Murray, PhD
Shirlee Sharkey

CONTRIBUTORS

Kyle Brown
Roy French
Madonna Gallo
Katie Hill
Fiona Hughes, MD
Paolo Korre
Kuhan Perampaladas
Lindsay Roxon
Jac Sanscartier
Maya Shapiro, PhD
Melissa Spellen
Patrick Glinski

EDITORS

Taylor Dennis
Esther Rogers

DESIGNER

Nayla Yehia

ADDITIONAL DESIGN

Pedro Marroquin

ILLUSTRATION

Jennifer Backman

Introduction

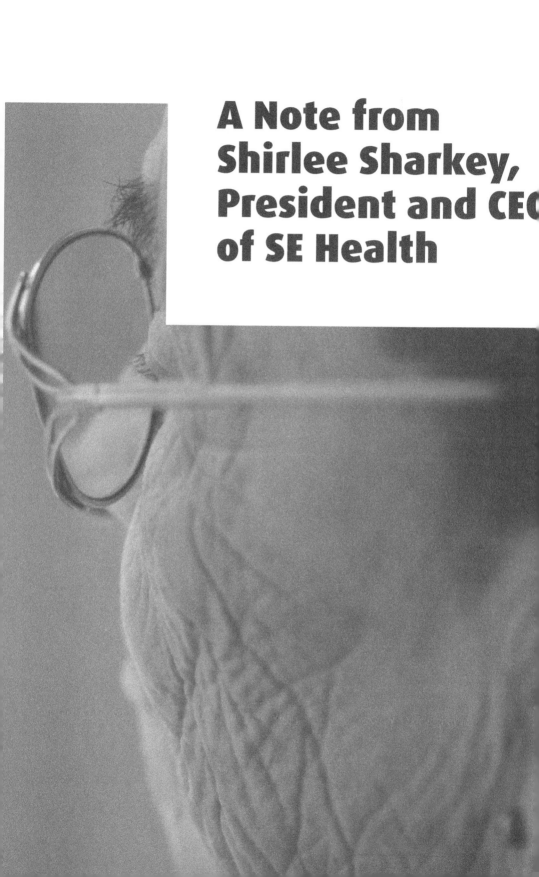

A Note from Shirlee Sharkey, President and CEO of SE Health

can't wait for you to meet Carrie! In Chapter Five, you'll be introduced to this vibrant and complex woman in her late seventies.
When we first meet Carrie at the beginning of the chapter, we see
a person who is tired of being patronized; she's frustrated by the constraints
placed upon her as an older woman, but she's also unsure about how to begin
revisiting her passions during her "fourth quarter." At the end of the chapter,
we get a glimpse of a reimagined Carrie, this time seeing a woman who has
been empowered to courageously explore long-forgotten parts of her life. By
leveraging technology and new models of care, Carrie is able to revisit important aspects of her identity—including her sexuality—and challenge who she
was, is, and will be. Her story paints a vivid picture of how aging adults could
defy expectations when given access to the right resources.

Carrie is one of the five personas you'll encounter when reading *The Future of
Aging*. These fictional characters are meant to capture the essence of what this
book is all about. Aging well is an expansive, important issue—one that goes
far beyond healthcare. The methods that organizations use to work with aging
adults, and the design solutions they create as a result, impact virtually every
aspect of society. At SE Health, our focus is on caring for people in their homes
and communities. We were drawn to this work because it reflects our desire to
solve the problems people face today, but it is also equally focused on uncov-
ering opportunities for tomorrow. This partnership with Idea Couture was a
"hand in glove" fit for us, and I'm pleased to share it with you. Our organizations are passionate about putting people first; we see humans, not organizations, as catalysts for changing assumptions about what it means to age, and
about who should ultimately shape how aging is experienced in the future.

The book comprises five chapters: Aging and Community, Health
Interventions, The Promise of Gerontechnology, Economic Contexts, and
Identity. Each chapter covers the current realities and future possibilities
around its core theme. Combined, these chapters represent a complex, holistic
view of what it means to age, and what it takes to age well. The book's flexible design means that it could be used as an extensive stand-alone resource,
while the individual chapters could also be leveraged by different audiences.

Each chapter begins with a set of insights that capture the current experiences
and challenges facing older adults. It then shows how these challenges can be
overcome through a set of foundational shifts—that is, large-scale transitions
taking place within society today. These shifts are anchored by signals, which
are cutting-edge examples from across the private and public sectors, including academic, health, and industry-specific organizations. These groups are
already doing the hard work of making the world a better place for aging
adults. The robust, engaging research informing each chapter helps this
work strike the balance of evidence-based content that is also accessible,

fun, and informative. A very cool example of this can be seen in a section of Chapter 3: The Promise of Gerontechnology, in which the persona from this chapter uses home monitoring extensively. This isn't science fiction—most of the technology described throughout the book already exists. It is very exciting to think that, in the not-too-distant future, new technology and systems will work to positively impact the lives of older people everywhere.

Certainly, emerging technology will play a pivotal role in the future of aging. When it comes to considering potential solutions for the challenges that seniors face, we need to start in the right place. Rather than adding new layers of technology, the people and organizations designing these solutions should pause and think through how technology can *complement*, rather than *complicate*, people's lives. For example, as my own mother aged, we found it easier to simply leave the television on all the time, because Mom often pushed the wrong buttons and lost her channels. When I think about this in the context of today's technology, I consider the multiple chargers, software updates, and interfaces that many of us—regardless of our age—find challenging to navigate. It's important to remember that new solutions should be designed in a way that considers such possibilities, as poor usability can have broader human implications. The fact is, older adults want to engage with technologies—they just need to be brought into the process of designing in the first place.

This book also examines the personal, cultural, and social needs of aging adults. Seniors, like most people, have an innate desire for a sense of belonging; for the ability to make their own choices regarding their identities and relationships; and for respect from those around them. This book further explores these needs—including how we are failing to meet them—using data and global examples. We hope that such exploration will inspire conversations around how we can support aging adults to live independently and make their later years rich and meaningful.

This book will leave you Spreading Hope and Happiness®, our vision at SE Health. With its refreshing tone, exploration of real-world solutions, and analysis of significant challenges facing the aging population, *The Future of Aging* offers a great balance of knowledge and humanity. Looking closely at the different issues we explore in this book—like the myth of living longer, the importance of maintaining one's sense of self, and the experience of isolation—inspired me to look at the future that I want to build for myself. I soon found myself thinking about my identity, which is inextricably tied to my work at SE Health. This led me to consider the possibility of my future retirement. It strikes me as odd that the transition from working to retirement is a hard stop, unlike so many other life transitions. For example, the role you play in raising your children changes as your family ages, and physical changes (including most ailments) occur gradually over time. It seems possible, then, that the abrupt end of a person's work life might contribute to feelings of loneliness, identity issues, and even depression. I can't help but to reflect on how we might improve this transition: How can we enable retired adults to keep their spark, to continue growing, and to find new ways to shine a brighter light on society?

Contemplating this issue and its relationship to other challenges has me thinking, believe it or not, about interlocking toy bricks, like LEGO®. The issues that aging adults face comprise many different parts of one interconnected experience—just like a partially constructed LEGO® tower. Many parts of the tower have already been built, but some loose pieces still remain. Some of the sections have already been attached to the base of the tower, while others have yet to be incorporated. It seems like an enterprising child could sit down on a rainy Sunday and transform this chaotic construction zone into one complete, fully connected model. But the beauty of LEGO® is not just that it's possible to connect things—it's the infinite number of combinations that are possible. This level of personalization can serve as a metaphor for good design, as it teaches us that our solutions must be flexible and adaptable. When it comes to the experience of aging, there is certainly no one-size-fits-all answer.

All of this is to say that many of the innovations, ideas, and devices described in this book already exist. Many are well-designed and constructed; now, it is time to connect these disparate parts to build a cohesive, interactive system that will improve the quality of life for aging adults, now and in the future. We are very close to this future state, but completing the final stages of construction will mean working together. By collaborating with individuals and organizations across different areas of expertise, we can build a lasting and flexible structure that will benefit each of us long into the future. And what an exciting future it will be.

Shirlee M. Sharkey
President and CEO, SE Health
CHE, MHSc, BScN, BA, LLD (honoris causa)

Redefining What It Means to Age Well

What comes to mind when you think of an older person? Who are they? Where do they live? What does their day look like? Perhaps, like many others, you see something like this:

A slightly hunched man in his seventies or eighties sits in an armchair. He wears slacks, glasses, and a worn-out sweater. The man uses a walker to get around the retirement home he resides in, where the staff know him as being friendly and genial, though often forgetful. Someone always reminds him when it's time to head to the dining room for meals, and a nurse brings him his pills at breakfast and dinner— all generic options covered by his insurance. She leans in close as she places the small cup of pills next to his plate, and she speaks loudly into his ear so that he can hear her voice over the bustle of the dining room. He watches old TV shows, fumbles to understand how to use the smartphone when his grandkids try to FaceTime, and generally distrusts or ignores new technology.

Once a week, his daughter visits with her family. She presses him about medication, worries about his health, and tends to assume that he should just "listen to his nurses and doctors." His grandchildren smile respectfully as he recounts stories they've all heard plenty of times before: tales of the job he has long been retired from; the cottage that he can no longer climb the steep steps to visit; and the wife, their grandmother, who has been gone for five years. He often mixes these stories up— proving, at least to his family, that he is both in decline and stuck in his ways. Mealtimes and weekend visits aside, the man spends most of his time sitting in his room, lost in thoughts of the past and out of tune with the world around him.

This portrait is a familiar one. You've seen films and read books about this man; he may even bear some resemblance to someone in your life. Yet despite the truths it may touch upon, this image is far from a complete depiction of what it means to be an aging adult today, nor is it a detailed look at how this experience is changing. Aging, after all, is not a singular process. There are

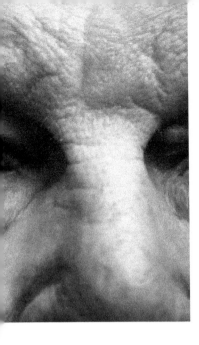

How can we begin to reimagine social systems and infrastructure, to implement training for skills and capabilities, and to create products, services, and technologies that will improve the lives of people getting older longer?

many overlapping—and often conflicting—social, emotional, and physiological dimensions that complicate what it means to age.

The habit of associating aging with illness and decline is borne not from malice, but from a lack of experience with diverse aging populations. After all, the rate of life expectancy at birth has been rising exponentially since the early 1900s, having nearly doubled from just 47 to 77 in the US. This three-decade increase has completely altered what it means to live well and live together. In other words, today's older adults are living longer, on average, than anyone ever expected them to—and society is not prepared for this change.

As a whole, individuals and institutions lack appreciation for the powerful implications that longer lifespans have for all aspects of life. Increased longevity presents profound challenges—and also incredible opportunities—for a diverse range of industries, government agencies, communities, and individuals. We must respond to the challenges by asking: How can we begin to reimagine social systems and infrastructure, to implement training for skills and capabilities, and to create products, services, and technologies that will improve the lives of people getting older longer?

We currently think of older adults as passive actors, rather than active

participants in the world, and this stigma and prejudice shapes how we understand, engage with, and design for this group. But aging is more than a process of diminishing health and mental acuity, and it is not defined by a loss of physical, social, and financial independence. It is also more than just a period in which people fall into static routines, behaviors, and worldviews. Rather, aging is a dynamic and evolving experience, one through which the contours of health, wellness, identity, politics, technology, and socioeconomics are constantly challenged by shifting needs and desires.

There are many emerging design challenges for those who provide services and products for the aging population. These go far beyond the goals often associated with aging: that is, overcoming the economic challenges of an increasingly large and unwieldy population of older adults, and developing cost-effective future healthcare interventions. The latter focus is particularly understandable, given that $1 trillion is spent on healthcare for elderly Americans each year. Still, there are many opportunities across other sectors of the economy—including for media and technology companies, lifestyle professionals, social media and app developers, apparel designers, architects, healthcare organizations, government agencies, and so many other stakeholders—to work from a more holistic frame of aging rooted in 21st century ideas. These organizations can use new models of collaborative design to create new policies, services, products, technologies, living

spaces, and even approaches to shaping intergenerational communities—all of which could be transformative for the lives of older adults.

These are among the many rich and provocative topics covered in *The Future of Aging*, all of which offer unprecedented opportunities for organizations globally. The vision proposed in this book is intended to help shape a holistic understanding of well-being that will ultimately support older adults in living well—and on their own terms—across all aspects of life. With this understanding in place, individuals and organizations can position themselves as long-term partners in navigating ever-evolving experiences of aging. These actors can contribute to a rich, complex aging experience that is the natural ground for exciting new innovations, partnerships, community initiatives, lived environments, and ways of connecting people.

In other words: The next time you're asked to imagine an aging person, we hope that you won't quite know where to begin.

Motivations and Methodologies

The Future of Aging is the result of a partnership between Idea Couture and SE Health. Together, we wanted to present a counter-argument to the common thinking and discourse around aging put forth in academia, business, and popular culture, where emphasis is frequently placed on a few very limited topics: the burden and cost of an aging population, the prevalence of loneliness and sickness in this group, and the experience of dementia. The focus on economic burden, in particular, has led to ageist metaphors like the "silver tsunami" appearing in various publications, from *The New England Journal of Medicine* to *The Economist*. Such language limits the role of older adults to one of dependence—a role that is transactional and devoid of agency. Further, it reflects a certain level of surprise on the part of analysts, most of whom have

failed to account for aging adults up until now.

In contrast, we crafted the content of this book using the method of strategic foresight. This method is used to capture emerging trends across different social, political, economic, and technological contexts. In addition to using foresight methods to map trends in how aging is understood and engaged with, we conducted a series of expert interviews with leaders in private and public sectors from across North America and Europe to support our mapping exercises. The resulting work calls attention to the limits inherent to current approaches to aging, while also offering exceptional examples of leaders who are working to overcome these limits in the urban development, healthcare, digital technology, financial, government, and social service sectors.

We explore imaginative future worlds in *The Future of Aging* using personas: that is, stories grounded in ethnographic research that reveal how overarching themes may play out for a particular person. In each chapter, we first explore the challenges that a specific person might face; then, after exploring signals of change tied to these challenges, we revisit this person to suggest an alternate future. By closing each chapter in this way, we intend to showcase a future free of ageism, prejudice, and dismissiveness. Here, aging is no longer seen as an inevitable process of loss and decline that is defined and shaped by the monotony of passing time. This vision also reflects a commitment to countering narrow-minded, fear-mongering questions around caring for the elderly, reducing the economic burden they pose, and maximizing their independence; it does so by offering constructive solutions to the challenges of today and tomorrow, in an evidence-informed way.

More than anything, this book is meant to help diverse stakeholders craft a better future for aging adults. We ask: How can these stakeholders partner with older adults to discover and create new meaning in their lives? How can they support older adults in embracing the dynamic and evolving dimensions of aging? How can they help people continue to build new, engaging, and caring relationships—to feel connected, yet still independent? How can they build technology into the experience of aging to help individuals live on their own terms?

We hope that *The Future of Aging* will serve not as an endpoint, but as inspiration for readers to begin a much larger conversation around how we can realize better futures for the aging population, today and in the future.

Overview of *The Future of Aging*

This book is organized into five chapters. Each chapter highlights a key aspect of the experience of aging, then explores the challenges and opportunities that an individual or organization might encounter when working with older adults to build a better future.

Though each chapter can be read on its own, the book itself represents the richness and complexity of what it means to get older. Together, these chapters reflect a holistic understanding of aging—one in which community, healthcare, technology, identity, and financial well-being are not siloed, but are viewed instead as entangled threads that hold equal importance for building a better future of aging. Each chapter is structured as follows:

A systemic perspective that brings to light dominant ways of understanding and engaging with the experience of aging, as they relate to the chapter's theme.

A set of **experiential insights** uncovered during our research, which help us explore specific challenges tied to the chapter's theme. These are followed by an **anchoring persona**, which helps bring these challenges to life.

Signals of change, which we use as inspiration for how these challenges may be addressed in the future.

A set of **design strategies** for overcoming obstacles, tensions, and emerging concerns that will impact how stakeholders across different industries grapple with the chapter's overarching theme. These are followed by a **future scenario**, in which the persona introduced earlier in the chapter benefits from solutions inspired by the signals.

Chapter 1: Community examines how living spaces and communities are changing. We explore what it means to live well with others. This chapter focuses on emerging concerns around community and urban development, as well as new spaces and models for home-making, healthcare, and creating health and wellness. It also addresses the informal systems that will come to play an important role in supporting healthy aging in one's community, and in providing agency to "live in place" and even "thrive in motion."

Chapter 2: Healthcare Interventions addresses problems with placing too much emphasis on biomedical interventions as the key to life extension and health management. This chapter focuses on emerging trends that privilege less formal and clinical approaches to care—approaches that help people take ownership of their health and wellness journey, and that treat individuals as people rather than patients.

Chapter 3: Gerontechnology is about the unique ways in which older adults engage with new and emerging technologies to help them maintain independence, restore and manage their health, and build and maintain new social connections. The chapter balances what might be technologically possible in the future with what will ultimately be desirable to individuals as they shape their own experience of aging.

Chapter 4: Economic Contexts challenges long-held assumptions about work, spending, retirement planning, and investment. More than anything, this chapter tries to highlight the value of breaking down the linear ways in which society tends to think about life stages and long-term planning.

Chapter 5: Identity reveals and seeks to overcome the troubling ageism that persists in how people understand and engage with aging adults. The chapter emphasizes shifts in how older adults are coming to think about their bodies, minds, relationships, sexuality, and mortality as fluid.

CHAPTER ONE

Aging and Community

SYSTEMIC

PERSPECTIVE

Where Individual Meets Environment

Understanding the current state.

"Although some of the variations in older people's health reflect their genetic inheritance, most is due to their physical and social environments, and the influence of these environments on their opportunities and health behavior."

World Health Organization, *Facts on Aging and the Life Course*

The World Health Organization (WHO) defines "healthy aging" as the process of developing and maintaining functional ability that enables well-being in older age. There are three elements comprising functional ability: the capacity of the individual, the environment the individual inhabits, and the interplay between these two spheres. This chapter focuses on the second component, environment. Specifically, it looks at the role that one's community has in helping them maintain health and well-being in later life. An individual's community encompasses their health and social systems, as well as their physical environment, all of which are considered important intermediaries to healthy aging.

Social Determinants of Health

Between 2015 and 2030, older populations— defined by the United Nations as those over 60 years old—are expected to grow by 41% in North America and 23% in Europe, alongside even more rapidly aging populations observed in Asia, Africa, and Latin America. With this aggregate shift in demographics, governments are beginning to examine how their growing aging populations may come to challenge the sustainability of their health systems. Many want to transform these systems, which represent the single largest budget line for most governments, by transitioning from a costly focus on acute care beds to a comprehensive system where health is created and maintained in the community.

This massive reorganization—which aims to reduce the footprint of inpatient spaces and increase investing in infrastructure for outpatient spaces, such as home and community—is happening in countries such as Denmark, where the acute length of stay is currently 3.5 days (versus 6.5 days across the Organisation for Economic Co-operation and Development [OECD]). The country also plans to further reduce length of stay by deinstitutionalizing care delivery, and allocating more budget to the community care sector.

New community-based models of care are also emerging, such as Health 1000 in the UK, a primary healthcare practice for older adults with complex health and social needs. Also in the UK, Age UK developed an Index of Well-being in Later Life to look at how older adults rate their well-being across domains and how various factors contribute to it. The Index reinforces the central role of community, as it emphasizes the importance of older adults maintaining meaningful engagement with the world to bolster their well-being. These initiatives challenge predominant medical models of aging.

Many health systems are dealing with the need to address not only the immediate health issues of an aging population, but also the failure of society to address the underlying causes of disease that have compounded over time. According to the WHO's Department of Aging and Life Course, though individuals may start with similar health statuses at birth, their paths diverge over time as "inequalities accumulate over the life course, due to exposure to multiple health, environmental, and social risks or barriers." For example, according to an article published by the Gerontological Society of America, relationship status in older adults—that is, whether they are married, never married, divorced, or widowed—is a significant determinant for long-term care admissions.

In this chapter, we look at how various emerging community models, built environments, and informal systems will come to play an increasingly important role in supporting healthy aging in one's community.

"The hyperlocal context becomes more important for the vulnerable. For seniors and children, you need the things that will keep [them] well in [their] community and close to home."

Alexis Wise, Director of Health and Human Services at Sidewalk Labs, Excerpt from Expert Interview

The Five Domains of Well-Being in Later Life

PERSONAL
Covering living arrangements, family status, caring and helping, intergenerational connections, and thinking skills.

SOCIAL
Covering social, civic, creative, and cultural participation as well as neighborliness and friendships, and personality attributes.

HEALTH
Covering physical and mental health, mental well-being, long-standing illness or disability, diagnosed health conditions, and physical activities.

RESOURCES
Covering employment status and earnings, pension income, financial and housing wealth, home ownership, and material resources.

LOCAL
Covering satisfaction with medical, leisure, public transport, and shopping services.

EXPERIENTIAL

The Experience of Social Clustering

Exploring the context of community

"It may be in the cultural particularities of people—in their oddities—that some of the most instructive revelations of what it is to be generically human are to be found."

Clifford Geertz, "The Impact of the Concept of Culture on the Concept of Man," *Bulletin of the Atomic Scientists*

Communities are unique and dynamic combinations of individuals, places, ideas, and practices. They are cultivated by people who share a space, have common interests, take part in activities together, and participate in both giving and receiving support—all of which creates a sense of purpose, belonging, and stability among community members.

Throughout a person's life, they forge communities at various scales comprising family, friends, colleagues, and neighbors. These different groups then come to form the social safety net that individuals rely on for emotional and physical support. This support is a critical determinant of overall health and well-being at any age, but its form undergoes radical transformations across multiple transitions that occur in later life.

In this section, we examine how older adults' social relationships, cultural values, and built environments impact their personal beliefs, attitudes, and needs, which then drive their daily decisions and overall life satisfaction. We provide a brief overview of some established social and cultural factors that come together to shape how older adults engage in and experience community as they age. Finally, we identify and imagine how emergent forces of change might reshape community for aging adults in the future.

Belonging

The effects of chronic illnesses, declining mobility, or living on a fixed income cause many older adults to disengage from the social activities that they previously enjoyed. As they retreat from the extended communities offered by clubs, associations, or teams, they also lose the social bonds that have provided them with a sense of belonging. Meanwhile, disruptions to living arrangements—such as moving into an intergenerational household, a retirement home, or a healthcare facility—engender a greater

Throughout a person's life, they forge communities at various scales comprising family, friends, colleagues, and neighbors. These different groups then come to form the social safety net that individuals rely on for emotional and physical support.

need for belonging, as well as a desire to understand one's role in society. Shared housing offers the possibility of new relationships, but it may also set the stage for loneliness, as a loss of independence and a sense of being away from one's "real" home can lead to isolation or depression.

Current models for engaging aging adults in organized communities focus on providing medical and emotional support, but few consider how to appeal to older adults through their personal interests and values, or through the knowledge and skills that they can contribute to the community. Developing community models that specifically address older adults' sense of belonging means discovering who people are and providing the support they need to form new social connections.

"Social relationships are consistently associated with biomarkers of health. Positive indicators of social well-being may be associated with lower levels of interleukin-6 in otherwise healthy people. Interleukin-6 is an inflammatory factor implicated in age-related disorders such as Alzheimer's disease, osteoporosis, rheumatoid arthritis, cardiovascular disease, and some forms of cancer."

National Institute on Aging, *Research Suggests a Positive Correlation Between Social Interaction and Health*

"Independence doesn't mean being alone; it means being able to manage and get access to the things you need on your own. Community means somewhere where it's easy to create informal connections."

Helene Martel, Director
for Elder Care & Palliative
Care at Kaiser Permanente,
Excerpt from Expert
Interview

Purpose +

Status

Older adults experience many changes in social status and identity, which are brought on by life-course events like retirement or watching children and grandchildren move away. These changes are often linked to a lost sense of self-worth or purpose, particularly for people who have spent most of their lives within a social and economic environment that aligns "productive capabilities" with identity and personal value. As they become less responsible for others and less likely to contribute to their communities in the ways they once did, older adults may come to feel less like capable people.

Typical programs and services for people of all ages are designed according to the principles of individualism and productivity. Because such initiatives promote the value of standard status symbols like wealth, high-powered work, physical fitness, and other forms of achievement that do not align with old age, they allow discrimination against elderly people to emerge and persist.

Moving forward, programs and services should be designed based on an understanding of the diverse and elaborate ways people can contribute to society. This would allow older people to be responsible, find purpose, and achieve social status in ways that they had previously not considered.

"Ageism: A process of systematic
stereotyping or discrimination
against people because they are
old, just as racism and sexism
accomplish with skin color and
gender. [...] Ageism allows the
younger generations to see older
people as different than themselves; thus they subtly cease
to identify with their elders as
human beings."

Robert N. Butler,
Age-Ism: Another Form of Bigotry

Programs and services should be
designed based on an understanding
of the diverse and elaborate ways
people can contribute to society.

Loss +
Transition

The traditional role of family as the social safety net for older adults is being challenged, with marital instability, financial pressures, and geographic dispersion making it increasingly difficult for older adults to access adequate support from their partners, children, and siblings. At the same time, today's older adults are living longer with chronic health issues, which means they may need more support than ever. As they spend less time with their adult children, and as their partners, family members, and close friends pass away, many older adults need to make deliberate choices about which community they will choose to support them as they age.

New ways of building community through both formal and informal systems of support are emerging to create stability for older adults experiencing loss and declining health. Alternative ideas and models of community can help promote resilience among older adults as they navigate the relationship transitions and losses that come with aging.

"Elderly individuals who have lost a spouse are four times more likely to live in an older adults' residence or nursing home compared to those whose spouses are living."

Statistics Canada, *Transitions to Long-Term and Residential Care Among Older Canadians*

John's Story

Bringing to life current challenges in community.

To help bring to life the concepts explored throughout this book, we have created personas for each chapter. A persona grounds ethnographic research within an individual narrative and reveals how overarching themes may play out for a particular person.

The persona for this chapter is John, whose story is intended to bring to life insights about the challenges older adults face as they try to make connections and shape meaningful roles for themselves within their communities. At the end of the chapter, we will see another version of John's story: one in which some of the possibilities discussed throughout this chapter have been enacted, resulting in an improved community experience for John.

John is a 75-year-old man who lives alone. He has been a widower for two years. John was diagnosed with type 2 diabetes in his fifties, and he has experienced moderate osteoarthritis for about five years. He has hired a part-time care-giver from a home-care service to help him complete tasks around the house, and to keep him company. John often wishes that he had a wider support network, but he doesn't know how to integrate into a new community.

The story below represents a brief glimpse into John's daily life, including the challenges he faces coping with a missing sense of community.

John took a slow sip of coffee as he turned the next page of his book, then breathed in a gust of crisp morning air. The leaves fell steadily from the trees lining John's quiet street; it was that same frigid breeze that slowed John down each day. Massaging his stiff hands, John glanced over at the empty chair beside him, trying not to think about how lonely the past year had been. At least his home-care aid, Nikita, would be arriving soon.

With all of John's close family members living hours away, Nikita was the only companion he had. He rarely spoke to his only child, Michael, who had become distant since John's wife Katherine passed away, and who frequently traveled for work. Moreover, while the people on his street seemed nice, he couldn't seem to develop meaningful relationships with any of them—the only interactions he could manage with these far younger strangers were distant smiles and quick hellos. Whenever they spoke on the phone, Michael suggested John go out on dates, but he wasn't looking for romance.

As he noticed Nikita pulling up in her old, rickety sedan, John closed his book and drained the last of his coffee. She looked exhausted as she got out of her car and walked to his door.

"Morning, John," she said. "Is that your favorite book again?"

John nodded and smiled as he stood with the help of his cane. Sometimes, if Nikita wasn't in a hurry to get home to her family, John would read her a passage from *Walden*. However, whenever he discussed the appeal of living in the woods—a desire he had shared with Katherine—Nikita would simply nod. He sometimes wondered if Nikita was really listening or if she was just humoring him.

He had been spending so much time alone since Katherine passed. His moments of solitude, which he had once treasured, had become an inescapable state of isolation. Katherine had always been the one to make plans, like visiting the nearby lavender farms or having dinner with friends and family. Without her, he was having a hard time knowing who to reach out to—and how.

Later that afternoon, Nikita drove John to the nearby shopping plaza to pick up some groceries. John sighed as he noticed a group of joggers passing by.

"I used to do a five-mile run with my colleagues while I was working in insurance, no problem, you know," John said. "We wouldn't even get out of breath—we'd just talk and joke around the entire time."

"I'm not much of a runner myself," Nikita replied, smiling at the familiar story.

John lightly tapped one of his knees. "Guess I'm not either these days."

As Nikita parked at the large plaza, John couldn't help but think about how much the world around him had changed. Many of the ads he saw were animated, and people walking by all seemed to be glued to their phones. He had a difficult time understanding people's values today.

John undid his seatbelt as the car came to a stop, then gestured to the woman walking by with a cell phone in her hand. "Can you believe everyone has one of these things?" John said, shooting Nikita a look of discontent. To his dismay, Nikita was typing away on her phone as well. John pretended not to notice.

Later that day, when it was time to say goodbye to Nikita, John tried stalling by asking her questions about how to work the washing machine. They both knew he just wanted to have someone to talk to a little longer, even though he had already paid for her to stay past what they scheduled.

He watched Nikita walk back to her car, the empty chairs on his porch in his periphery. Even though it was nice to have Nikita's company, something was missing. Later that day, John watched the sun set like always and daydreamed about spending time with people he could truly get to know—people he could laugh with and learn from, and who would see him as more than just an old man who needed help.

FORESIGHT
SHIFTS

Transforming How We Shape Meaningful Connections

The future of aging in one's community.

"We don't heal in isolation,
but in community."

S. Kelley Harrell,
Author

To understand how the aging population will come to redefine community, we must first identify and articulate "shifts"—that is, large-scale transitions that are taking place within society today. We use these shifts to help articulate the tensions that emerged during the foresight research phase of this book, during which we performed diverse scanning to identify the many changes influencing Western society. These changes come in many forms, including films, articles, emerging tech startups, and conversations. Shifts allow us to frame new questions and establish future-oriented points of view, which in turn enables us to imagine and create more meaningful realities for aging individuals.

SHIFT 1

From Predefined Community Models

to Creating Your Own Living Community

The elderly are beginning to proactively seek out more social living arrangements in order to form closer trusted circles where they can find both companionship and care.

"I mean, we're both alone. We've been by ourselves for too long. For years. I'm lonely. I think you might be too. I wonder if you would come and sleep in the night with me. And talk."

A widow to a widower,
Our Souls at Night

> A Home, Not Alone

Some insects, including a species of ants, don't deteriorate with age. These creatures care for their young and hunt and forage for prey even into old age, their brains remaining sharp until the end of life. Researchers have been unable to isolate the gene responsible for this anti-aging feat, leading them to speculate that the reason for the insects' continued vigor is social complexity: the fact that they live in highly organized colonies. Humans are strikingly similar social creatures. The social connectedness that comes from communal living is good for us too; it improves our mental and physical functioning, while social isolation (including isolation caused by physical immobility) is associated with higher rates of depression and dementia in older adults. The value of thinking in these terms is especially important when considering what are often called "elder orphans": that is, older people without a spouse or children on whom they can depend. They too need human connectivity to remain vibrant and engaged in the world around them.

"Loneliness increases the likelihood of mortality by 26%. More than nine million people in the UK report often or always feeling lonely, and roughly 3.9 million or two-fifths of all older people in the UK say the television is their main source of company. To create policies that address this sad reality of modern life, the UK appointed a Minister of Loneliness in 2018."

Campaign to End Loneliness, *Loneliness Research*

Seeking Unity in a Polarized World

The Brexit vote and Trump election in 2016 can in part be understood as reactions against globalization, with the tipping point being the millions of refugees displaced from increasingly volatile regions, such as Syria. Those supporting these movements may have been rooted in a sense of nostalgia and imagined security brought by the close-knit communities of the past, where most people knew each other, shared a religion, and had similar values as their neighbors. While the idealization of this past may be misguided, especially considering the discrimination inherent to such homogeneity, these social phenomena force us to acknowledge the real longing people have for spaces where they can congregate and feel part of a community united by a common purpose.

Today, older adults in search of a shared

Whether it's dorms in New York City, the women's only Babayagas' House in Paris, connected-living pods in Japan, or co-owned homes in suburban Toronto, older adults are rediscovering the benefits of housemates.

community outside the home are perhaps
more likely to gather at shopping malls or
via online forums than they are to meet in
spaces where they used to convene, such as
places of worship, labor unions, clubs, or
community-service organizations. Some
are going to even more extreme lengths to
foster greater social connectivity. Rather
than resigning themselves to the isolation
of living alone, or settling on a future of
bingo and jellied vegetables in a retirement
home with beige walls, they are rewriting
the rules around what living arrangements
for the old look like by getting roommates
or moving into intentional communities.
Whether it's dorms in New York City, the
women's only Babayagas' House in Paris,
connected-living pods in Japan, or co-owned
homes in suburban Toronto, older adults
are rediscovering the benefits of housemates. Having friends in close proximity
gives them someone to rely on for company
and support. Life transitions at any age
are difficult, but these events are easier to
manage if they are intended and planned for.
Rather than having a move precipitated by
a life crisis, such as an injury or illness, the
death of a spouse, or the discovery that one
has outlived one's savings, adults of all ages
can now proactively start shaping how they
intend to spend their golden years—and
who they'd like to spend them with.

"Our Oasis T.O. Experience
Lab builds community
through participatory
decision making. [...] The
seniors there decide what
types of programs are
initiated, who works there,
[and] how they're going to
spend their budget. Having
something like this to put
their mind to gives [the]
community a reason to
interact, it gives them a
context for engaging, [and]
it gives them permission
and a context for getting to
know each other."

Jen Recknagel, Senior Design
Lead, University Health Network
Open Lab, Excerpt from Expert
Interview

SIGNALS

#1

Co-Dwelling for Care

Whereas many spaces that support care in later life tend to focus on age and physical ability, the Babayagas' House in Paris is based on common interests. Developed and run by a group of older activists, the house is a collective for women who are looking for camaraderie and who want to live (and die) within a supportive community. The group obtained government funding for a 6-story building that accommodates 21 women on the condition that the residents would all care for each other, meaning they wouldn't need care workers or state-run homes. The women all take care of the space together, and they also pool resources for formal healthcare services, such as appointments with clinicians.

#2

Safe Communal Spaces

Security and safety are a top concern of older adults when considering where they can and want to live. They have growing levels of uncertainty and volatility in the social, psychological, political, and economic environments. This is opening opportunities to design the next generation of safe age-friendly spaces. Across many rural areas in the US, declines in civic infrastructure—whether governmental or religious—have created a vacuum for spaces of social support and communal gathering. Older adults often meet in "safe" places like Starbucks and McDonald's to replace the public spaces of the past. In the future, as malls become less commonplace and social spaces become increasingly privatized, there will be a need for new types of facilities that allow older adults to connect with one another in new ways.

SHIFT 2

SHIFT 2

From Isolated and Alone

Older adults, their children, and their grandchildren are navigating how to live together as they find themselves relying on each other for financial support, as well as for physical and emotional care.

"Constant interaction with other people can be annoying, but overall seems to keep us engaged with life."

Thomas Perls, Professor at Boston University School of Medicine, Interview with *The Atlantic*

to Multigenerational Living Arrangements

West Meets East

While nuclear households are the most common family model in North America, many non-Western countries have long held multigenerational living arrangements as the norm. Over the next few decades, the growth of the aging population will lead to new types of living arrangements that offer better financial security for extended families. Today, in North America and Europe, multigenerational living arrangements are becoming more common; an increasing number of adult children are continuing to live at home, while elderly parents are packing up their homes and moving in with their children to share housing and help with childcare.

"Since 1997, the number of young adults (aged 18–34) living at home with their parents has increased by nearly 19%."

US Census Bureau

> Seeking Collectivity in an Individualistic World

Real estate developers are designing multi-generational homes in an attempt to address the spatial constraints that arise when older parents move in with their children, and when adult children continue living at home. In these housing models, features such as separate entrances and living quarters allow different generations to live independently under the same roof. When done properly, this type of arrangement allows for financial stability and a two-way flow of care and emotional support.

For example, grandparents who live with their children's families can care for younger grandchildren during the day or after school, eliminating daycare and nanny costs. They may also be able to perform school runs, or to simply connect and communicate with their grandchildren more consistently than the working parents can. Elderly parents, on the other hand, may find that living with their adult children enables them to receive extra help with activities of daily living, such as heavy lifting, maintenance, mobility, and medical support (driving to appointments, help with medications, etc.).

As more families are juggling work and family care, intergenerational living arrangements such as these can help relieve stress for the "sandwich generation": those struggling to care for both their children and their elderly parents (and, of course, themselves). Achieving greater interdependence through cohabitation appears to be an ideal choice, at least in concept. However, designing for the lifestyle considerations of different household members is key to creating functional spaces that balance the need for both autonomy and assistance.

SIGNALS

#1

Minimalist Modular Living

Innovative housing solutions are emerging that aim to increase older adults' participation and affirm their important role in society. One solution is the building of small senior-friendly homes, sometimes clustered together or located on the property of the residents' children or caregivers. These modest structures, which appeal to retirees looking to downsize, are known as laneway houses, coach houses, tiny houses, or accessory dwelling units. Living in these smaller homes can help support older adults' need for independence and mobility, as well as their desire for connection. For those older adults who can still manage stairs and who like to travel, tiny homes can double as RVs and be placed on the back of a trailer. In the UK, Australia, and parts of the US, backyard "granny flats" are becoming increasingly popular, as they help to better integrate grandparents into family life.

#2

Resilient Caregivers

Almost 75% of the care of older adults in the US and Canada is provided by family caregivers. Public and private healthcare providers are recognizing that family caregivers have not been given the needed attention nor support commensurate with their vital role in the outcomes of older adults in their care. Family caregivers often risk becoming invisible second patients due to the stress, anxiety, and financial hardship associated with caregiving. In an effort to increase felt ownership, and to give family caregivers a greater role in decision making about how care and support are delivered, the Australian government recently introduced the Home Care Packages Program on a consumer-directed care basis. As part of the country's Aged Care Reform, this program gives older Australians and their family caregivers access to four levels of government-subsidized services in their homes, depending on the level of need. In this "self directed" model, the older adult and their family have agency over what types of care and/or services they'd like support with, how and when these are delivered, and by whom. The services could include formal care, such as a home-care aide, but could also include services such as a gardener or housecleaner. This shift toward reablement-focused home care is allowing a greater number of older individuals in Western countries to benefit from support in their homes, rather than in institutions. It also emphasizes the importance of the active involvement and support of caregivers, which leads to greater caregiver resilience.

SHIFT 3

From Informal Systems of Care

to the Formal Caregiving Economy

Ensuring a sustainable care economy needs to be less about increasing efficiencies and improving productivity, and more about valuing the work of informal caregivers, thereby improving access to emotional and physical support for those in need of care.

"The question is not 'Do I want a robot companion to care for me?' but 'Would I accept being cared for by a robot?'"

Geoff Watts, "The One-Armed Robot That Will Look After Me Until I Die," *Mosaic*

> Labor of Love

It's inevitable that many individuals will
require extra care and support as they get
older—someone to help them clean, get
to healthcare appointments, or to manage
bathing, for example. Whereas families
have long been the locus of care for the
old and infirm, today, adult children often
live far from their elderly parents and/
or are too busy with work or raising their
own children to provide care. Spouses with
aging partners, who may be coping with
health issues themselves, aren't always able
to provide the care their partner needs.
Many become burnt out from the constant
demand. With more elderly people than
ever before in need of care, the issue of who
should provide caregiving support—and
how—is ripe for a rethink.

"**The in-home senior care
market in the US was
worth an estimated $80
billion in 2015.**"

AARP, *Caregiving in the
United States*

Seeking Regulation in an Informal World

The caregiving role traditionally fulfilled by family members is being increasingly filled by paid caregivers. Often, these workers are women from developing countries such as the Philippines—often mothers themselves who have left their own families behind. In North America, such workers represent one large, underpaid group that provides care for the elderly. Recognizing that home care represents a huge market that is constrained by the availability of labor, health technology startups like Hometeam in the US and Elder in the UK now offer personalized and on-demand services to help the elderly easily get matched with paid caregivers to help with everyday tasks, including nursing or companion care. In Japan and Sweden, emerging technology companies are experimenting with robotic pets and housekeepers to support older adults in the home. Outside of the physical realm, virtual home companions are beginning to simulate distinct human personalities based on the complex AI-based algorithms that underpin them. These technologies designed to augment traditional labor-based home care are growing in function and popularity; soon enough, we may see digital companion chatbots making conversation with the elderly while robots care for their physical needs.

While robots are being used to help fill the caregiving gap, distortions in the human caregiver labor force are emerging and often go unrecognized. The global economy has created care chains in which

the elderly in industrialized countries receive care from labor-sending countries at the expense of the elderly (and children) in the care providers' home countries. Like childcare, eldercare has traditionally constituted domestic—and therefore invisible—labor done largely by women. Today, this important work is still socially and financially undervalued; in many cases, it is also still unregulated, making caregiving a low-paying job with high turnover. Further, while robotics may offer a solution to the home-care labor shortage, the potential monetary benefits of mechanized companions must be weighed against the social costs. Rather than giving older adults greater independence, robot solutions may threaten older adults' already fragile sense of control. Mechanized companions are getting closer and closer to building empathy and trust, and they are becoming better at engaging in human contact and communication. Yet, they still lack a number of human qualities that lie at the heart of care. Even if they come to possess these qualities, collaborative engagement with their human counterparts will be necessary.

Like childcare, eldercare has traditionally constituted domestic—and therefore invisible—labor done largely by women. Today, this important work is still socially and financially undervalued.

#1

Countering Skin Hunger

Healthcare practices have become increasingly dehumanizing; complex human systems have been reduced to tasks to be performed by specialized health professionals, who merely seek to eliminate dysfunction. We are now beginning to see a shift away from this mechanistic, materialistic, "body parts" approach to the care of the elderly. For example, some psychologists now recognize the existence of "skin hunger." Defined as the need for physical contact, skin hunger left unchecked can result in emotional, mental, and even physical implications. Professional cuddling agencies, such as Cuddlist.com, are beginning to pop up to meet the wide variety of intimacy needs people have. And this is not just a North American phenomenon—the business of cuddling is gaining popularity all over the world. In Japan, for example, "cuddle cafes" are known as *soineya*, or "sleep together shops."

#2

Carebots

Professor Kate Devlin of Goldsmiths, University of London, believes the future of robots in eldercare will include fulfilling the desire older adults have for human intimacy. Softbank Robotics's Pepper is the first humanoid robot capable of recognizing human emotions and adapting its behavior to the mood of its interlocutor. Based on voice, facial expressions, body movements, and choice of words, Pepper interprets emotions and offers the appropriate type of content or interaction for the given moment. Meanwhile, interactions with the robotic seal Paro, one of the most widely studied therapeutic animal-robots, have been shown to increase motivation, improve mood, and reduce stress in elderly people. Japan is already ahead of the carebot market for older adults by about 10 to 20 years—but will Western society adopt the same devices to provide companionship and care for their elderly?

SHIFT 4

From Offline Relationships

As digital platforms become the dominant medium for communication across socioeconomic, geographic, and age-based barriers, the diversity of those using technology to connect on-to-offline will come to redefine what connection means.

"People leave traces of themselves where they feel most comfortable, most worthwhile."

Haruki Murakami,
Dance Dance Dance

to Connecting Everywhere

Friends in New Places

Social connection gives people opportunities to communicate, which improves their mental health and reduces loneliness and depression. While these conditions are by no means limited to the elderly, they certainly afflict older adults as partners die, friends move away, and busy families struggle to find time for them. While today's youth are digital natives, older adults are stereotypically viewed as reluctant, clumsy tech adopters—latecomers to the world of the internet. However, as engagement with social networks increases among the general population, so too will the number of elderly people logging on to expand their social networks grow.

"A study revealed that among older adults, nearly half (48%) of 70–74 year olds are using social media, and more than a quarter (28%) of 96–99 year olds are online."

"Study Reveals Trends in Older Adults' Internet, Social Media Usage," *LeadingAge Washington*

> Seeking Intimacy in an Unfamiliar World

Older adults are increasingly turning to the internet in their search to grow new friendships and extend their social lives. They are connecting with others via social media apps, such as Instagram and Facebook, and sites geared toward older adults seeking companionship, such as Senior Chatters, Over Fifties Friends, and Stitch. Social network algorithms help connect older adults to other people with similar interests (or even similar health concerns), allowing them to chat when they're lonely or bored and to exchange stories and health tips.

These networks are especially important for older adults with mobility issues, as they allow them to connect with others and to check in with their families more frequently. For her *New York Times* article "Online, 'A Reason to Keep on Going'," Stephanie Clifford interviewed many older adults who said that learning to connect with others online brought new meaning to their lives.

While there are many benefits to connecting virtually, people still require physical places where they can nurture their relationships. Expressions of self-disclosure, vulnerability, and empathy still work best face-to-face. In her 2011 book *Alone Together*, Sherry Turkle, a professor of Science, Technology, and Society at MIT, warns that we should resist the temptation to conflate the benefits of virtual interactions with real face time, noting that "it is possible to be in constant digital communication and yet still feel very much alone." Given our "phygital" lives, in which our on and offline identities are increasingly interconnected, at issue is perhaps less the question of the advantage of one way of being over the other, and more the question of how to extend online connections into opportunities for in-person relationships.

SIGNALS

#1

Digital Company

Hoping to provide company to those dining alone, an Osaka-based ramen chain developed a promotion that allowed diners to eat a meal alongside a virtual companion. The restaurant provided patrons with a QR code that gave them access to one of five videos starring popular Japanese musicians eating ramen alongside in-store patrons. VR company Rendever also seeks to give older adults virtual access to parts of the world that they're missing. Their technology creates an environment where they can hike up Machu Picchu as a group, go on a walking tour of Paris, or work together to recreate Picasso's masterpieces—all without leaving their homes.

#2

Meal Sharing

Feastly, EatWith, Dinner Surfer, and Cookapp are all mobile apps that seek to facilitate local supper clubs with strangers. They aim to connect people over meals, unite people in a world of increasingly detached social interactions, and limit food waste. Several municipalities in countries like China, the United Arab Emirates, and Spain are also experimenting with the concept of community fridges: publicly placed fridges where local citizens can donate unused or leftover food for others to access.

Bringing the Future of Community to Life

Building out possible concepts and solutions.

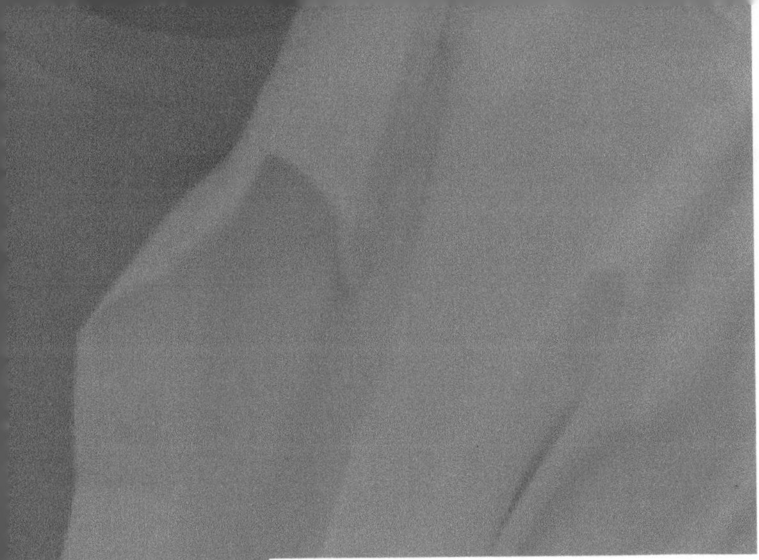

"Even on the smallest material level, complexities have been revealed in which we are the ones who are excluded and remote. Thus an inquiry into our location is more productive than ever, as it examines the place that humans create in order to have somewhere they can appear as who they are."

Peter Sloterdijk,
Professor at the
University of Art and
Design Karlsruhe, from
Spheres Volume 1: Bubbles

The sweeping social, economic, political, environ-mental, and technological changes that are already underway today will inevitably reshape how older adults like John experience aging within their communities in the future. Despite these radical shifts, the human need to depend on and connect with others—during times of transition and when negotiating the challenges of everyday living—will remain. For many, the goal needs to be the development of what Bruce Sterling has called a "gerontopia": that is, cities, villages, and communities that emphasize the agency and vitality of older adults as a primary design goal. While some older adults will continue to thrive socially despite changing circumstances, namely by relying on their own sociability or strong communi-ties to find and foster meaningful relationships, many others will struggle with social isolation and loneliness as they age. To minimize the latter possibility, and the mental and physical ramifications that often result, we must consider the drivers of positive and healthy relationships for older adults when envi-sioning the ways in which they will continue to foster a sense of community as they age.

EXPERIENCE DRIVERS

Forces Influencing How Older Adults Experience Community

To create services and experiences that support older people in planning for their future living models, we must consider their shared concerns from a range of class and socioeconomic backgrounds. This also entails factoring in the experiences of the people who surround seniors, such as their family and close friends. The experience drivers below summarize some of those concerns. They also provide points of departure to keep in mind when imagining ways to ease tensions and improve processes and outcomes for older adults in the future.

1. Living Arrangements

Older adults struggle with the prospect of having to give up their position as masters of their own domain, but they also fear that living at home alone could lead to an absence of help when they need it most.

> How might we help older adults reconcile their desire to live independently with their need for a sense of security and belief that support will be readily available if needed?

2. Community Models

Community provides older adults with a sense of belonging, and it also engenders a sense of purpose as they work to create, shape, and sustain the social group to which they belong.

> How might we provide opportunities for older adults to take an active role in building new kinds of communities based on shared priorities?

3. Systems of Care

Reciprocity is a key part of forming social bonds. To feel less dependent, older adults seek ways to give back to fellow community members, including formal caregivers.

> How might we help older adults identify and share their skills and knowledge in order to build deeper connections with other members of new communities?

4. Social Spaces

Many older adults have localized social lives. For this reason, they often want to get out and participate in the activities and events offered in their neighborhood or community.

> How might we enable participation in communities beyond the block for older adults who live in areas lacking local events and activities?

OPPORTUNITY SPACE

Rethinking Community and Investing in the Right Community-Development Initiatives

Given the systemic, experiential, and foresight perspectives brought forward, as well as the learnings we captured in our interviews with aging and healthcare experts across North America and Europe, we have defined an opportunity space as a takeaway for this chapter. We use opportunity spaces to capture the key thinking and findings uncovered in our research. These spaces are also intended to inform and inspire organizations across industries to design better futures, in this case, for older adults.

This chapter's opportunity space calls for industry actors and innovators to leverage their unique position to respond to the social and community needs of an aging population.

Invest in Congruence

Context

In a world that can feel polarized and lonely, aging adults seek a social life and space that is highly compatible with their emotional needs.

Opportunity Space

Organizations should explore opportunities to promote feelings of agreement and harmony in communities designed for older adults.

Though most people value having meaningful relationships and being members of long-lasting communities, their ability to do so is constantly challenged by disruptive events, including personal and environmental changes. To create communities based on harmonious, mutually beneficial, and rewarding relationships, organizations will need to understand which factors affect compatibility—particularly in the long term.

Today, organizations have new opportunities to design more harmonious living arrangements, community models, care systems, and social spaces for older adults. To take advantage of such opportunities, these organizations must define new value propositions, develop new decision-making processes informed by data and AI-enabled systems, and deploy new business operating models that reflect an informed understanding of the nuances of relationship and community building.

When they are able to take into account the key factors that affect social compatibility—including belonging, purpose and status, as well as loss and transition—stakeholders across the housing, social services, caretaking, and community-development industries will be empowered to create meaningful spaces for older adults to age, both today and into the future.

Reimagining John's Story

Throughout this chapter, we explored the current realities and challenges facing older adults in the context of community-building. We also traced some emerging trends and signals that are pushing us beyond current models of community and toward new living arrangements and lifestyles.

In closing, we would like to reimagine John's story to explore some of the powerful ways that forming unique connections with a diverse community might have a profound impact on his life. In this version of John's story, the importance of connecting with people from different backgrounds comes to the fore, as does the value of living in a space designed for his unique needs. This doesn't mean that all of John's problems are solved, or that he is happy all the time; rather, this lifestyle gives John a sense of purpose while empowering him to know when, who, and how to ask for help.

Andre handed John another cup of coffee, then sat in the chair next to his. "You know, you should probably start drinking decaf," he said. "Your gut will thank you."

"What, you think my wife didn't remind me of the same thing every day for 30 years?" John asked, smirking.

Just as Andre was about to respond, he was interrupted by a loud cough from the other room. Both men looked up in alarm as their other roommate, Daniel, launched into yet another intense coughing fit. The coughing had been going on for nearly two weeks, and Andre and John were getting concerned.

After the coughing subsided, Daniel walked into the kitchen. His face was flushed, and he avoided eye contact with his roommates as he said good morning and grabbed a mug from the cupboard.

"Dan, have you—" John began, but he was quickly cut off.

"It's fine," Daniel responded abruptly. "I'm fine. I made an appointment with the doctor for this afternoon, so I don't need either of you giving me any more grief. Okay?"

John knew better than to be put off by his roommate's gruffness. Daniel was a lifelong bachelor with a stubborn, proud exterior, but over the past year, John had seen Dan's softer side. John suspected that this response had less to do with wanting to be left alone, and more to do with being afraid that this lingering cough might be a sign of something more serious.

"We're giving you grief?," John said. "Before you came in here, Andre was lecturing me on the dangers of regular coffee. Between his nagging and your defensiveness, it's like being married all over again."

Daniel sat down at the table with his coffee. "Sorry John," he said. "I'm just tired. I feel like I haven't slept in weeks."

"You haven't," Andre chimed in. "And neither have we, with all that coughing. What, you think we want you to go to the doctor for your own well-being? We're not that selfless."

"That's true," Daniel chuckled. "Don't know what I was thinking."

The three men sipped their coffee in silence. Andre scrolled through the feeds on his phone and John flipped through the paper, but Daniel just looked out the window absent-mindedly. John noticed that his roommate was chewing on the side of his thumb, which he sometimes did when they were talking about something that made him nervous—like dividing the household bills, for example, or even going on a date.

John broke the silence. "All right, Danny-Boy. You've talked me into it: I'll drive you to your damn appointment."

Daniel jumped slightly at the abrupt announcement. "What? No, that's okay, John. I don't need—"

"No need to argue," John interrupted. "You've already convinced me. I had a very busy day of reading planned, but I suppose I can make time."

Daniel looked down at his coffee and tried to conceal his small, relieved smile. He chuckled as he took another sip, then suppressed another cough. "Thanks John," he said quietly.

John flipped to a new page of the paper and pretended to be absorbed by an article. "Anytime, my friend."

Health
Interventions

The Limits of Biomedical Intervention

Understanding the current state.

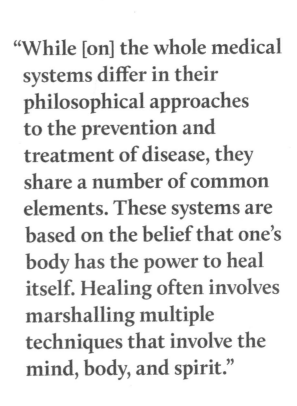

"While [on] the whole medical systems differ in their philosophical approaches to the prevention and treatment of disease, they share a number of common elements. These systems are based on the belief that one's body has the power to heal itself. Healing often involves marshalling multiple techniques that involve the mind, body, and spirit."

Syed Amin Tabish, "Complementary and Alternative Healthcare: Is It Evidence-Based?," *International Journal of Health Sciences*

Today, aging is largely seen as a problem to be over-come. This problem, many fear, will be exacerbated by people living longer and requiring greater access to healthcare services, spaces, and treatments. There is a perception that the excessive draw on healthcare will generate a catastrophic ripple effect—especially when it comes to creating an increased demand for already scarce healthcare workers, and to the building of new, more technologically robust institutional settings for care.

Yet, this "problem" of aging is framed around narrow understandings of what health is and how it can be achieved. Many healthcare practitioners (HCPs), pharmaceutical companies, healthcare facilities, and other actors are still committed to a biomedical understanding of health—one that privileges the clinical expertise, practices, and settings of medical professionals. The rise of professional medicine in the 19th century brought with it the promise of science- and evidence-based approaches to treating and curing disease. This mindset emerged alongside the enormous spread of hospitals as "houses of cure" through the 19th and mid-20th centuries. It is clear why healthcare today still revolves around resisting, curing, and eliminating disease.

Yet, this emphasis on medical expertise has given way to a new mindset over the last half century, one that is even more focused on the technological and scientific aspects of health. Those promoting this perspective imagine the future of healthcare to be one of more technical precision, more efficient institutional spaces, and an increasingly microscopic and molecular understanding of what makes each person unique. Social scientists like Adele Clarke, Professor Emerita of Sociology and History of Health Sciences at the University of California, San Francisco, often refer to this as the era of biomedicalization, where the goal is not just the extension of life, but the transformation of it through scientific and technological intervention.

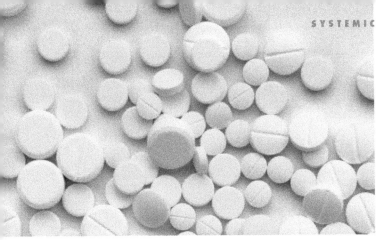

The Treatment Orientation

Perspectives about aging are influenced heavily by our biomedicalized world. There is a certain level of decline in physical strength and mental acuity associated with the aging process. Loss of vision and hearing, changing cognitive abilities, and altered motor functions are all normal and accepted aspects of aging. Yet, even these natural events have been biomedicalized, making it difficult not to conflate normal aging with the biomedical assessment, treatment, and cure of actual diseases. If there is no cure for aging, then why do we talk about it as though it's something we can eliminate?

A partial answer is that the "cure" imperative is embedded in both popular imagination and current healthcare systems, which are designed for acute care of treatable illnesses. In this model, healthcare journeys follow a narrow and linear path: After experiencing symptoms, an individual consults with doctors and specialists. Following these consultations, which often involve a series of tests, the person receives a diagnosis. The

person—now identified first and foremost as a patient—eventually gets on the best possible treatment plan, which either succeeds or fails to cure their condition. Of course, this process is never so simple; people, their loved ones, and their HCPs do a lot of work to negotiate the complex social, emotional, and physiological realities of healthcare intervention. Yet, this model persists. When it comes to aging, this focus on outcomes makes it very difficult to consider the broader dimensions affecting the health and wellness of older adults.

Just as the aging population is growing rapidly, so too is the prevalence of chronic illness—particularly in North America. Current healthcare models are not prepared to deal with long-term disease experiences that, rather than being linear or predictable, are instead characterized by fluctuating symptoms, evolving treatment plans, and complex comorbidities. Like the aging process, chronic diseases actively resist standard models of care, in part because

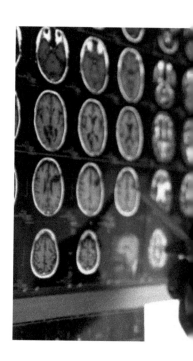

they impact every aspect of someone's life. The longer someone lives, the more likely they are to experience at least one chronic condition, though they are more likely to receive multiple diagnoses. Despite an increased awareness around "multi-morbidity"—that is, the occurrence of multiple chronic diseases—most healthcare systems continue to place emphasis on treating each disease separately. This approach leads to serious problems, including "polypharmacy": the practice of being prescribed and taking multiple medications for one or several diseases. Polypharmacy can make it nearly impossible for some individuals to adhere to their prescribed treatment regimen, and as such, it poses significant safety risks, including increasing the likelihood of falls, hospitalization, side effects caused by unexpected drug interactions, and even death.

Older adults may prefer not to take these risks. If given the opportunity, many might choose instead to take advantage of complementary practices for health and healing. However, the default "treat and cure" approach means that alternative options are often left off the table entirely. The imperative to diagnose, treat, and cure can lead to overscreening and overtesting—including screenings and tests that pose their own risks and few benefits. Healthcare facilities around the world have begun implementing specialty-specific "Choosing Wisely" campaigns designed to identify redundant and unsafe prescribing and testing. Yet, these initiatives have come up against critical backlash from players in the medical and pharmaceutical sectors, who have accused these campaigns of encouraging rationing.

When it comes to confronting the hyper-medicalization of aging, the challenge is not in eliminating or diluting the influence of medical expertise, which is and will remain critical to effective healthcare. Rather, the challenge is in limiting the extent to which biomedical knowledge and interventions are privileged over other approaches to wellness, aging, and chronic illness. As Pulitzer Prize-winning historian of medicine Paul Starr once put it, "By shaping the patients' understanding of their own experience, physicians create the conditions under which their advice seems appropriate." People are increasingly recognizing

the limits of biomedical expertise; many are beginning to view biomedicine as one part of a larger constellation of health and wellness practices, techniques, and environments. As such, they are seeking proactive solutions and prevention. These individuals are motivated to take ownership of their health and wellness, and to determine what role biomedical interventions should play in their lives.

When it comes to confronting the hyper-medicalization of aging, the challenge is not in eliminating or diluting the influence of medical expertise; rather, it is in limiting the extent to which this knowledge is privileged over other approaches to wellness, aging, and chronic illness.

"Health and wellness should be one of many factors that help people make decisions in their lives. At the same time, people shouldn't stress themselves out about everything they're not doing perfectly, as though they can ever know what perfect might be. [...] We need to stop people from waking up every day and feeling inadequate, because that stress can undo a lot of the other work they are doing to get well. We need people to understand, for instance, that they can actively change their blood pressure—they do have some control."

Doug Roth, Heart and
Stroke Foundation, Excerpt
from Expert Interview

Intervention Beyond Healthcare

The stigma around being old—and therefore "in decline"—is consistently reinforced, especially in affluent countries. Dr. Todd Nelson of the University of California, Stanislaus, has called this "prejudice against our feared future self." This phenomenon, he notes, is in direct opposition to attitudes around aging present in many other cultures—especially Indigenous communities around the world, where older adults are revered and respected. Rather than deride and dismiss elders for their physical and cognitive decline, these cultures elevate the value of older adults by actively seeking to learn from and engage with their knowledge and lived experiences. This appreciation is rooted in a non-linear view of time: Because aging is not viewed as a one-way process of physical and mental decline, people find it easier to appreciate a more complex interconnection between young and old. In contrast to this, Western thinking around aging creates and recreates this divide, resulting in ageist ideas and attitudes that are difficult to overcome. Older adults are seen as being dependent upon healthcare systems, rather than capable of actively shaping their personal health narratives. Further, this thinking precludes any possibility of older adults empowering others—whether young or old—to take ownership of their health and wellness.

Throughout the rest of this chapter, we will explore some promising complementary ways of thinking about health and wellness, including practices, attitudes, and interventions that could be used to help reframe aging as a vibrant, vital process to be embraced rather than a problem to be overcome.

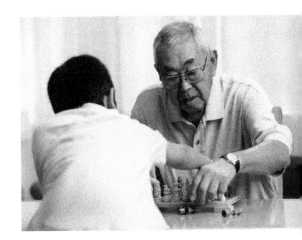

The Experience of Negotiating with Age

Exploring the context of intervention.

"...the way we live is only one among innumerable ways of life which humans have adopted. If we glance sideways and backwards, we will quickly discover that modern society, with its many possibilities and seducing offers, its dizzying complexity and its impressive technological advances, is a way of life which has not been tried out for long."

Thomas Hylland Eriksen, *Small Places, Large Issues: An Introduction to Social and Cultural Anthropology*

Stigma +

Every day, forward-thinking people and communities develop new ways to anticipate and adapt to the physiological, mental, and emotional requirements of healthy aging. As we begin to explore emerging shifts in health-care interventions, it is important to call out more specific attitudes, beliefs, and practices that continue to be influenced by the biomedical model. These include stigmas associated with aging and the idea of aging successfully, as well as emotional experiences of aging, and how these experiences intersect with assumptions and practices around how best to treat people. Finally, we must consider the ways in which assumptions, beliefs, and values around aging can be altered in the contexts of both chronic illness and preventative healthcare. Combined, these insights represent the platform from which we can begin to identify and imagine alternative beliefs, attitudes, and practices in the future.

"Successful Aging"

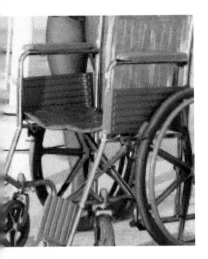

The biomedical model of healthcare depends on clearly defined terms, categories, and areas of specialization. While they are useful for managing specific diseases, such definitions and categories can be very dangerous in the social and cultural contexts of life. Though it is possible to clearly diagnose a disease, there is no way to predict how that disease will be experienced as an illness. It is easy, though not useful, to conflate the experience of symptoms with a person's interactions with their family, workplace, community, and broader society. This can lead to stereotyping and stigma, and the same is true when it comes

The experience of developing a chronic condition, losing mobility, or simply inhabiting a visibly old body is especially challenging in a society where personal worth is inextricably tied to the perceived health of body and mind.

to viewing the experience of aging as insep-
arable from that of disease. An older person
with a disease is often limited by assumptions about what they can and can't do,
which in turn affects their overall ability to
engage with the world around them.

Conspicuous physical and cognitive
changes can make it very difficult for aging
adults to take control of their own sense
of health and wellness. The experience
of developing a chronic condition, losing
mobility, or simply inhabiting a visibly old
body is especially challenging in a society
where personal worth is inextricably tied to
the perceived health of one's body and mind.
Many older adults reject the notion that
successful aging means retaining a certain
amount of physical and cognitive strength;
however, other approaches that seek to
complement (if not to supplant) biomedical
approaches to aging well still overemphasize
functional abilities. Such approaches often
value the capacity of older adults to contribute to society in conventional ways.

"**Research suggests those with
undiagnosed, 'mystery' illnesses
account for up to half of all visits
to family doctors and approximately 15% of specialist appointments, reporting ailments that are
often surprisingly common, such
as migraines and lower back pain,
that can't be traced to a medical
cause.**"

Erin Anderssen, "Their Pain Is Real—
and for Patients with Mystery Illnesses,
Help Is Coming From an Unexpected
Source," *The Globe and Mail*

"In my world, when I think of prevention, it's around things like dementia. We still don't have treatments for it. I'm thrilled there continues to be lots of research into vaccines and cures, but what do we know so far, in terms of ways to hopefully stave off dementia as long as possible? It's things like social isolation—people need connections—[and] good sleep, good nutrition, and physical activity. These are the pillars of prevention, for any health issue. We need to continue to find ways to expand people's access to these things, whether or not we have a cure."

Helene Martel, Kaiser Permanente, Excerpt from Expert Interview

Emotional
Regulation +

Resilience

One way to overcome the limits of current approaches is to take the emotional experience of aging more seriously. There is now compelling evidence that emotional functioning actually improves as people age. Research suggests that older people experience negative emotions less often, because they can be more selective about the social contexts they choose to engage with, and they also have a more developed ability to manage and respond to emotional experiences. Resilience is a capacity that is built up over the course of a lifetime, and it begins with an individual's ability to regulate how they feel and act in response to positive and negative emotions. Older adults who have developed a healthy mindset and behaviors for coping with challenging emotions earlier in life are even better equipped to cope with the challenges of aging.

Even among those who have a well-developed capacity for emotional regulation, circumstantial factors still impact how a person copes with and recovers from stressful situations. An individual's perception of their ability to control their own experiences is critical to their emotional wellness and resilience. When worsening health conditions, financial circumstances, or other factors lead older adults to feel like they are losing control over their life, body, or sense of self, the risk of hopelessness—and even suicide—increases. While older adults are demanding new attention be paid to issues such as the choice of when and how to end one's life, it will take time to alter the social and cultural ideas about end-of-life decisions. It is important, therefore, that we consider not just how to help people develop the awareness and tools for cultivating individual resilience early on, but that we also contend with how different circumstances in later life may warrant different kinds of responses.

"In two studies, we examined how individual variation in the ability to modify emotional expressive behavior in response to evocative stimuli is related to well-being and financial success. Study 1 showed that individuals who can best suppress their emotional reaction to an acoustic startle are happiest with their lives. Study 2 showed that individuals who can best amplify their emotional reaction to a disgust-eliciting movie are happiest with their lives and have the highest disposable income and socioeconomic status. Thus, being able to implement emotion regulation strategies in the laboratory is closely linked to well-being and financial success."

Stéphane Côté, Anett Gyurak, and Robert W. Levenson, "The Ability to Regulate Emotion Is Associated with Greater Well-Being, Income, and Socioeconomic Status," *Emotion*

Habits

People's habits, tastes, attitudes, and even knowledge about the world are the result of their cumulative life experiences within particular cultural and environmental contexts.

Aging adults have spent their lifetimes developing habits that are rooted in their understanding of the world around them. While habits provide older adults with reliable tools for confronting everyday challenges within their known context, they often get in the way of their ability to adapt to new knowledge, practices, and environments. This is especially true in the context of healthcare. Older adults often have entrenched ways of thinking about and engaging with HCPs and facilities, as well as long-held assumptions about treatment and healing practices. These entrenched ideas often conflict with both the realities of chronic illness and emerging movements signaling change—particularly those looking to provide greater agency to individuals and their loved ones when it comes to navigating their healthcare and wellness journeys.

As new attitudes, spaces, and practices alter the contours of health and wellness, aging adults need to be empowered to adjust their habits and routines, but also to know when they should privilege their own knowledge and experiences. More work needs to be done to help older adults break habits that may hinder their health or happiness, but also to understand the circumstances in which these individuals should feel empowered to reject unnecessary change and intervention.

"...about 40% to 45% of what we do every day sort of feels like a decision, but it's actually habit. [...] As a behavior becomes a habit, as it becomes automatic, it moves into the basal ganglia, which is one of the oldest structures in our brain, and it's near the center of our skull. And when things happen in the basal ganglia, it doesn't feel like thought. That's why a habit feels automatic, is because it's happening in this part of your brain that, for all intents and purposes, from what we think of as 'thinking,' is completely exempt from that process."

Charles Duhigg in an interview with Justin Fox, *Habits: Why We Do What We Do*

Maria's Story

Bringing to life current challenges in intervention.

To help bring to life the concepts explored through-out this book, we have created personas for each chapter. A persona grounds ethnographic research within an individual narrative and reveals how overarching themes may play out for a particular person.

The persona for this chapter is a character named Maria, whose story is intended to bring to life insights about the relationships older adults have with health interventions. Here, we look at how the challenges discussed so far may manifest in Maria's life. At the end of the chapter, we will see another version of Maria's story: one in which some of the possibilities discussed throughout this chapter have been enacted, resulting in an improved experience of aging for Maria.

Maria is a 70-year-old woman who lives with her two daughters, Cecilia and Sofia, and her teenage grandson, Tony. She has been a widow for ten years. She was diagnosed with Parkinson's disease five years ago, and she has experienced hearing loss since her early sixties. Her family is loving and supportive, though sometimes overbearing; while Maria is open to trying different treatment regimens to achieve the best quality of life possible, her daughters seem determined to eliminate rather than accommodate her symptoms.

The story below represents a brief glimpse into Maria's daily life, including the challenges she faces when it comes to navigating her healthcare choices.

Maria frowned as she looked down at the medications in front of her. She held the bottles up to the light, her right hand trembling intensely, and tried to see what color the pills inside were. I took one of these last night, she thought to herself, and I should be taking another this morning. But which one? She thought about asking Cecilia or Sofia, but quickly decided against it: The last thing she needed was to have her daughters deciding that she couldn't handle her own medication anymore. In the end, she decided to take both. What could one extra pill hurt, anyway?

She heard a tap on her bedroom door. "Abuela? Are you up?"

"Yes, sweetheart," she responded. "I'll be out soon."

"Mom wants to know if you need any help," Tony said.

Just as Maria was about to respond, there was another loud knock at her door. Almost immediately, the door cracked open and Cecilia poked her head in. "Ma? You okay in here? Need help getting out of your PJs?"

"I'm fine, Cecilia," Maria said, trying to conceal her irritation. "Give me five minutes, please."

"Sure, no problem. How's the hand today? New drugs helping at all? If you don't notice any difference, I can make another appointment with Dr.

Lockhart."

"I just took them, so we'll have to wait and see."

Ten minutes later, Maria made her way to the kitchen, where the rest of her family was already seated. She felt stiff and foggy, but she put on her most convincing smile as she sat down for breakfast. "Good morning!" she said brightly, wishing desperately that she could do something to conceal the tremor in her voice.

"Morning, mama," Sofia said as she placed a plate of scrambled eggs in front of her. "Cee and I were just talking about that trial Dr. Lockhart mentioned yesterday. I looked it up last night, and I can't believe how promising it seems. It sounds like they're actually making a real breakthrough in slowing the progression of PD."

"Yes, it's very exciting news," Maria said, cautious not to show too much enthusiasm. She stared at her eggs for a moment. She knew that as soon as she picked up her fork, one of her daughters would notice her tremor.

"Especially for dementia," Cecilia added.

Maria chewed her breakfast slowly and deliberately while her daughters discussed the logistics of her participating in a clinical trial. The mere thought of joining the trial made her feel exhausted. A trial would mean more appointments, more doctors, and probably more pills—all things that Maria was hoping to avoid.

She often thought about the relationship she'd had with her daughters before her diagnosis. Her days used to revolve around taking care of her family. She had prepared most of the meals, given Tony rides to and from school, and attended his soccer games. Back then, her daughters had confided in her when they had problems, and the family had all celebrated each other's successes together. Nowadays, most conversations revolved around eliminating Maria's symptoms. Sometimes, she felt like all they talked about was Parkinson's.

"Anne called me last night," she interrupted. "She wanted to let me know that Ryan is back in hospital. Heart troubles."

Cecilia reached out and touched Maria's hand. "I'm so sorry, mama. I'm sure he'll pull through. Ryan has always been a fighter."

Maria smiled. "He's always been a feisty one, that's for sure. But I think he's starting to get tired of being sick. He's accepted that his time is here."

"Don't say that, mama!" Sofia interjected. "He'll be just fine. Don't you worry."

"Speaking of being fine—here, mama. Read this." Cecilia placed a booklet in front of Maria. She didn't have to open it to know that it was about the clinical trial they had been discussing.

Maria didn't respond. Instead, she looked down, pretending to read the booklet, thinking to herself, *But I wasn't worried, my loves. I'm not worried at all.*

FORESIGHT
SHIFTS

Transforming How We Negotiate with Age

The future of health interventions.

"The good thing about being old is not being young."

Stephen Richards,
Author

In order to help people, HCPs, other wellness professionals, and a range of other organizations collaboratively redefine the contours of health and wellness interventions, it is important to first identify and articulate "shifts"—that is, large-scale transitions taking place within society today. Throughout this work, we use these shifts to help articulate the tensions that emerged during our foresight research. We performed diverse scanning of various moments of change influencing Western society, whether those came in the form of a startup, film, article, or conversation. Shifts allow us to frame new questions and establish future-oriented points of view, which can in turn help us imagine and create more meaningful realities for aging individuals.

SHIFT 1

From Anti-Aging Interventions

to Affirmative Aging on Your Own Terms

Aging in a healthy way does not have to mean trying to be youthful by denying significant changes in one's body and mind. Instead, seniors who embrace their changing physical bodies and overall sense of self may be better equipped to see the benefits of aging.

"The ideal aging citizen is someone [who] remains youthful as long as possible, contributes to the economy as a smart consumer and as an active participant in productive activities, and stays healthy to avoid accessing healthcare and other public services."

Jacqueline Low and Suzanne Dupuis-Blanchard, "Zoomers to Geezerade: Representations of the Aging Body in Ageist and Consumerist Society," *Societies*

> Embracing Your Future Self

In Western societies, old age has long been considered a departure from the ideal. From Hippocrates' time through to the 19th century, illnesses associated with old age were understood to be the result of a natural increase in humoral imbalance in a person's vital fluids. Later, during the Industrial Revolution, the popularization of the "body as machine" metaphor made it easy to see old age as a period of decline and deficiency. The less efficient the machine was, the less valuable it became—both for the individual who had to live with this broken body, and for the society in which he or she was now a less productive contributor. More recently, aging has become pathologized; today, it is considered an illness to be prevented, cured, or perhaps even reversed.

66

"In 2015, Americans spent $13.5 billion on aesthetic procedures, according to a report from the American Society for Aesthetic Plastic Surgery. While not all of these procedures are specifically intended to turn back time, four of the top five nonsurgical procedures that year—Botox, hyaluronic-acid injections, chemical peels, and microdermabrasion—qualify as anti-aging treatments."

Danielle Friedman, "Is *Death Becomes Her* the Anti-Aging Parable We Need?," *The Cut*

From Shame to Ownership

Today, anti-aging is a multibillion dollar industry based on an all-powerful idea: To be healthy, happy, and productive, one must avoid aging and remain youthful for as long as possible. Youth, according to this perspective, is a commodity that costs both money and time to achieve. To this end, increasingly popular "prejuvenation cosmetic treatments"—everything from cosmetics, to foods, to pharmaceuticals, to personal computing devices—are sold with the promise that they can delay aging. However, there is a growing movement of older adults reclaiming aging by resisting the imperative to stay young. They are slowing down the treadmill and rejecting the challenge to perform physical and emotional feats that demonstrate their "fight" against getting old.

In response to the "successful aging" movement, which permits people to grow old only if they maintain the same needs, wants, and behaviors of their youth, many older adults are working to normalize the aspects of aging that too often represent stigma and embarrassment. They are embracing their need for hearing aids, for example, or being open about incontinence and constipation. They are also working to feel more confident as they live through chronic conditions that lead to serious mobility issues, or to the loss of bodily functions and mental faculties perceived as crucial for independent living. In short, many older adults are seeking to create space for open, visible acknowledgment of the many important aspects of aging. This behavior reflects the need for deeper and more meaningful conversations between seniors and their HCPs regarding their needs, desires, and experiences.

SIGNALS

#1

Building Healthy Optimism

When a group of seniors in the UK were asked to identify their role models for a survey, many chose people who don't try to conceal their age, and whose skills, knowledge, and approach to life were inspiring. Participants most frequently listed their parents, grandparents, friends, and mentors—people who they saw as confident and committed to active lifestyles, and who embrace their age and do not fear death. Another survey, conducted by psychologists William Chopik, Eric Kim, and Jacqui Smith, and reported in *Scientific American*, found a direct link between optimism (more specifically, having a positive outlook) and physical health. Their findings indicate that people who are optimistic about their age and their overall healthcare are less likely to experience heart disease or strokes, and they are more likely to quickly recover from the worst aspects of painful illness or injury. The researchers also suggest that 75% of what makes someone optimistic comes "down to [their] social influences, personal experiences, and active choices to be more optimistic."

#2

Disrupting Assumptions

A number of companies are actively engaging patients in new ways to advocate for their healthcare while also encouraging them to embrace the aging process. According to AARP, their #DisruptAging campaign offers "a place to have a new conversation—often funny, sometimes raw, always honest—about how we want to live and age." The initiative has been embraced by notable social work researchers, like Dr. Leslie Hasche from the University of Denver. #DisruptAging empowers individuals to own their aging experiences, but also to share and help others. By making this work public through social media, email, and other forums, AARP is actively pushing against ageism in novel ways. Hasche herself has been at the forefront of redefining academic categories like aging and disability, which often prevent people from feeling comfortable owning their healthcare experiences. In a recent paper in the *Journal of Human Behavior in the Social Environment*, Hasche and her colleagues argue for a new social model that pushes against the biomedical, instead generating "intersectional and inclusive" work that helps bridge perceived gaps between the medical, social, cultural, and emotional dimensions of aging and disability.

SHIFT 2
From Curing Disease

The old adage "we are born to die" is taking on new meaning. As we shift from a production and consumption economy to an experience and wellbeing economy, prevention is becoming a new kind of intervention. The different approaches that individuals and societies take for prevention may begin at birth.

"The main weapons in the prevention and treatment of disease and human carelessness will probably always be food and exercise."

Dr. Blake F. Donaldson,
Strong Medicine

to Adapting Healthier Lifestyles to Prevent Illness

The Case for Living Well

As healthcare systems continue moving toward preventive care, aging is increasingly becoming a major focus. Prevention is a multifaceted endeavor that looks beyond symptoms, diagnoses, and treatments; it requires a comprehensive, in-depth understanding of healthcare problems. Yet, solutions still often come from the top down, as experts continue to try and shape how people approach prevention. This causes a lot of confusion. New evidence emerges daily on the "right" amount of exercise or the benefits of this or that diet: Mediterranean, no sugar, lots of protein and high fat—or is it low fat, vegan, local, or raw? This abundance of information, much of which seems contradictory, has led to a push beyond individualistic models of care. People cannot be solely responsible for making decisions, but they need to be empowered to define their needs, and they should know when and how to seek support. From there, a wide support network is often necessary, as family members, HCPs, and wellness professionals work to collaboratively define the terms of what it means to make good decisions in all aspects of life.

"I love to walk. Walking is a spiritual journey and a reflection of living. Each of us must determine which path to take and how far to walk; we must find our own way, what is right for one may not be for another. There is no single right way to deal with late stage cancer, to live life or approach death, or to walk an old mission trail."

Edie Littlefield Sundby,
The Mission Walker

> From Biomedical Intervention to Lifestyle Engagement

In many scientific circles, the biological process of aging is often speculated to be the primary causative factor for many chronic diseases in later life. Until recently, most scientists believed that our genes held the secret to delaying and reversing aging and disease. While biology certainly influences the aging process, it is becoming clear that epigenetic factors also have a significant impact. "Epigenetics" is a relatively new term; it refers to the understanding that our environment controls gene expression, meaning that daily behaviors—such as what people eat, where they live, who they interact with, how much they sleep, and how often they exercise—cause chemical modifications that turn genes on or off. Based on this understanding, aging is likely the result of both outside stressors and an internal cellular process. To control aging and reduce the risk of disease, people are being encouraged to engage in healthy behaviors.

Demographers working to explore the dietary factors that influence longevity identified what they called "Blue Zones": areas in the world with an unusually high percentage

of centenarians. Although the food staples across these communities vary significantly, the dietary habits shared across these cultures include a tendency to eat simple foods (mostly plants) and to avoid overeating or eating late in the day. It is likely that centenarians from these communities have a highly diverse gut microbiota as a result of their high fiber, low animal protein diets.

Though new insights on the microbiome emerge daily, there is increasing evidence to suggest that our diets can help keep us healthy—or, alternatively, that they can feed chronic diseases, such as certain types of cancer. Research examining the right amount and intensity of exercise is likewise conflicting, but studies have consistently shown that regular exercise (e.g. walking, cycling, swimming, dancing, or even gardening) reduces the risk of disease and decline. Learning to manage stress is also good for an individual's health, with popular relaxation techniques including mindfulness practices and meditation. Sleep regulation and conflict resolution skills have also proven key to managing stress.

It's often not enough to appeal to people's sense of reason or to provide incentives for them to take care of themselves; a more effective approach to fostering long-term lifestyle changes is providing supportive environments where healthy lifestyle choices are modeled and reinforced. Even with this type of social support, however, achieving health in old age is a lifelong endeavor that requires knowledge, a long-term commitment, as well as access to good food and circumstances that permit one to attain the proper amounts of exercise, sleep, and sunlight.

SIGNALS

#1

Exercise in a Bottle

Research has found that 1,000 molecular reactions occur when people exercise. The identification of these reactions has paved the way for drug treatments that mimic the effects of exercise in people's bodies. Likewise, research suggests that nanoparticles could deliver drugs to specific parts of the body that turn bad fat cells into good ones that actually burn fat. The system has been tested with obese mice and was successful in improving the cholesterol and triglyceride levels of test subjects; however, it has not yet been tested with human subjects.

#2

My Microbiome

Several initiatives and companies are emerging that specialize in probiotics and healthy bacteria. Researchers believe that diets tailored to people's gut microbes could help limit the rise of diabetes, heart disease, obesity, and other diseases. Several companies offering gut-microbiome testing, including Viome and Ubiome, have emerged. Another initiative, known as the Personalized Nutrition Project, is collecting data and developing an algorithm to create optimal diets and nutritional programs for individual consumers. Product- and service-oriented companies like Mother Dirt, Farmhouse Culture, and Truth Bar also offer consumers probiotic-rich foods, beverages, and skin sprays.

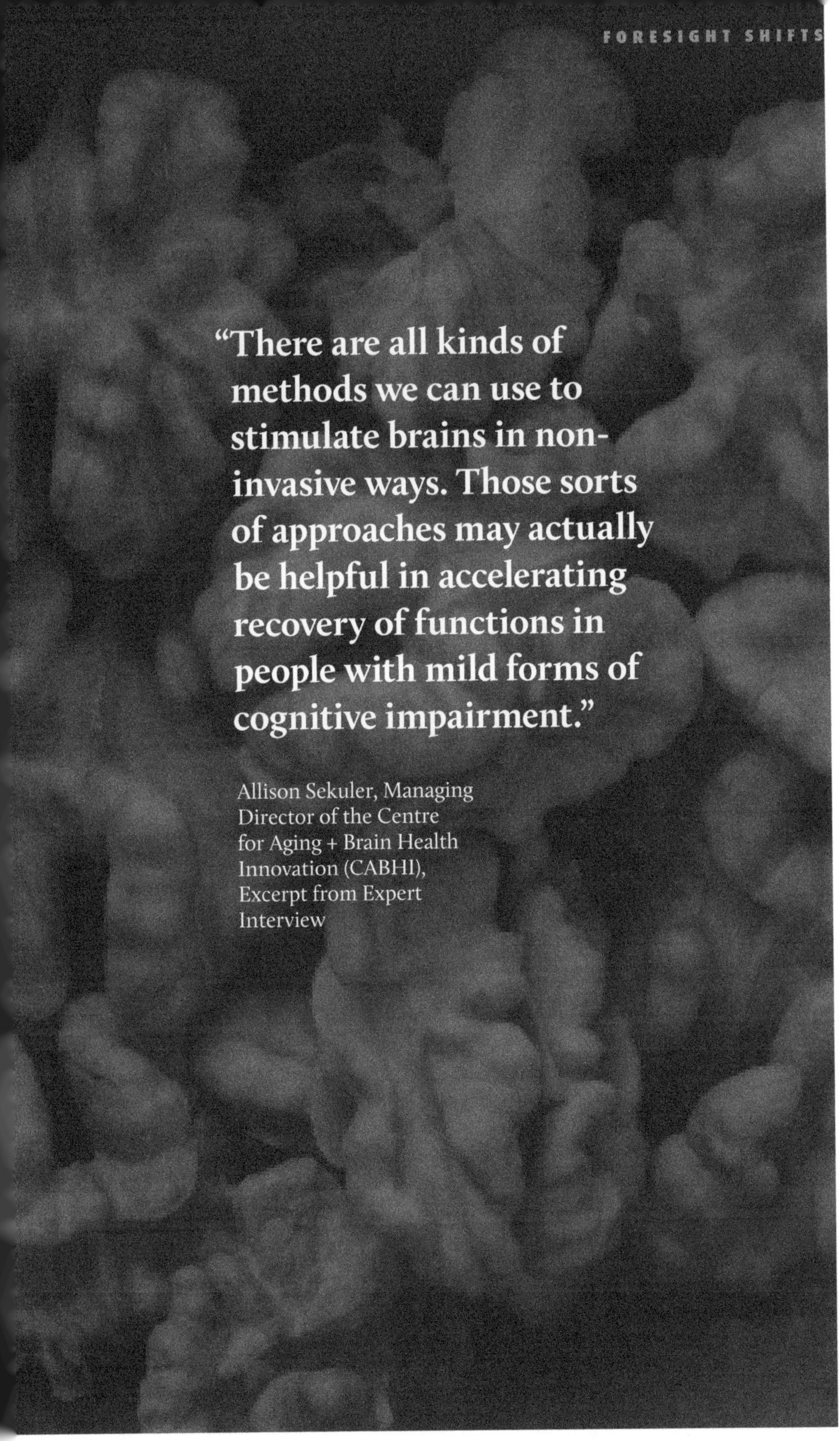

"There are all kinds of methods we can use to stimulate brains in non-invasive ways. Those sorts of approaches may actually be helpful in accelerating recovery of functions in people with mild forms of cognitive impairment."

Allison Sekuler, Managing
Director of the Centre
for Aging + Brain Health
Innovation (CABHI),
Excerpt from Expert
Interview

SHIFT 3
From Treating

While many aging adults mourn the loss of their abilities as they age, seniors can learn new skills—such as art, movement, and music—to help prevent, retain, and even improve their mental functioning.

66

"There is a fountain of youth: It is your mind, your talents, the creativity you bring to your life and the lives of people you love. When you learn to tap this source, you will truly have defeated age."

Sophia Loren

to Preventing Cognitive Decline through Neuroplasticity and Brain Re-Training

Mindful Care

Today, investigations into anti-aging therapeutics involve both the study of novel treatments and attempts to repurpose older medicines. Researchers at the Salk Institute in California have found a compound that can induce cells to behave like younger stem cells. Older drugs, such as the immunosuppressant rapamycin and the common oral antidiabetic metformin, hold promise for extending life and health span. Along with common supplements, such as human growth hormone, antioxidants, and vitamin D, a number of synthetic compounds (or "nootropics") are being marketed today as medications to improve cognition, recall, and focus. However, until more convincing evidence on the benefits of these various compounds emerges, some are choosing to focus on evidence-based practices that have been shown to prevent cognitive decline.

66

"Subjective well-being and positive affect are coupled to positive neuroendocrine, cardiovascular, and inflammatory parameters (Steptoe et al., 2014), confirming a tangible biological substratum for the long-suspected relationship between happiness and health."

Carlos López-Otín, Lorenzo Galluzzi, José M.P. Freije, Frank Madeo, Guido Kroemer, "Metabolic Control of Longevity," *Cell*

> From Rigid Theories to Contemporary Strategies

Neurodegenerative conditions are becoming more prominent among the elderly, greatly reducing quality of life in old age for many individuals. As Tony Wyss-Coray of Stanford University put it, "A failing brain is the arbiter of a death preceded by a gradual loss of the essence of being." While effective treatments for dementia remain elusive, research in cognitive neuroscience and neuropsychology has dramatically changed our understanding of the brain over the past decade. Researchers have learned that the brain, once thought to be a static, stable structure, is constantly shaped and reshaped

by our physical and mental activity. The brain frequently forms and reforms electrical circuits throughout each individual's life, making cognitive decline less an inevitable biological reality and more something that can be prevented or even repaired.

Neuroplasticity refers to the understanding that the structure and function of the brain is shaped by our behavior and movement, and growing expertise in this field is giving new meaning to the phrase "use it or lose it." Researchers have found that the brain's plasticity is enhanced when people challenge themselves mentally or physically. Contrary to popular belief, it isn't brain

games per se that keep individuals mentally sharp and physically agile into their eighties; instead, the key is to work hard at something—such as learning a language, an instrument, or how to play tennis or even bridge. The exertion required for mindfulness and contemplative practices has been shown to increase cortical thickness and gray matter, as well as to strengthen the areas of the brain that govern learning and memory.

The medical community continues to be surprised by the brain's capacity to heal itself. Using brain scanners, neuroscientists have tracked the changes that occur in the brains of those who meditate for just 30 minutes a day. Similarly, researchers are trying to understand what dancers know anecdotally: that while dancing, those with Parkinson's can move more fluidly. This research is making it clear that engaging in new ways of thinking and using the body, in spite of the challenges posed by aging, changes the brain for the better.

SIGNALS

#1

Advanced Cognitive Enhancement

Increasingly, cognitive-enhancement substances known as nootropics are being used in workplaces and schools to enhance an individual's ability to perform. The claim is that these substances improve cognitive functioning in a number of areas, including—but not limited to—mental alertness, anxiety, creativity, and memory. Substances that electrically stimulate the brain ("electroceuticals") may also be used in the future to enhance language and mathematical ability, attention span, problem-solving, memory, and coordination. While studies on efficacy are limited, these modalities could potentially expand options for the elderly to maintain or improve cognitive function, and allow them to individually experiment with solutions.

#2

Preventative Eating

In his book, *The End of Alzheimer's: The First Program to Prevent and Reverse Cognitive Decline*, neurologist Dale Bredesen introduces the Bredesen Protocol, which he claims has successfully reversed symptoms of cognitive decline in over 200 individuals. Based on his research, Bredesen theorizes that cognitive decline is due to inflammation and exposure to toxins, and to a shortage of brain-boosting nutrients, hormones, and molecules. The Bredesen Protocol evaluates and addresses 45 factors, but optimizing one's diet is an important piece. Bredesen recommends a mildly ketogenic diet in which sugar is eliminated. According to Bredesen, the brain benefits of a low-carb, high-fat ketogenic diet have been documented for many years now, as this diet forces the liver to produce ketone bodies rather than glucose, which is an optimal energy source for the brain. Healthy fats include olive, coconut, and avocado oils, as well as wild caught fish.

SHIFT 4

From Physical
to Emotional Determinants of Health and Healing

Emotions such as worry, stress, and resentment have been found to negatively impact longevity just as much as (or more than) physical imbalances such as high cholesterol and obesity. Some people are therefore choosing to place a greater emphasis on improving their emotional health by fostering feelings of gratitude, joy, and forgiveness.

"We know so much about how to adjust diet and how we eat, but we don't have a good framework collectively for our emotional health."

Robert Morris, in Kyle Vanhemert's "A Social Network Designed to Combat Depression," *Wired*

> How to Feel

While people in the past sought to drink from the fountain of youth, today, many are racing to find (or rebrand) the magic pill to cure aging. Global sales of anti-aging elixirs have topped $6 billion in recent years—an especially strange figure, considering the lack of scientific efficacy behind any of these products. While many believe that stopping aging and preventing disease is simply a matter of targeting the right genes, others are choosing to focus instead on other underlying factors, namely the emotional determinants of health and wellbeing.

❝❞

"We've spent billions of dollars in an effort to understand the molecular basis of Alzheimer's in the hope that it will lead to a cure, or at least to more effective therapies. And although we have greatly enlarged our knowledge of the disease, it has not yielded many successful treatments."

Clayton M. Dalton, "What Happened When Alzheimer's Patients Were Treated for the Diseases We Actually Have Cures for," *Quartz*

From Isolated Approaches to Integrative Practices

While many health factors are not subject to individual control, there are steps that any individual can take to improve their emotional health. In his book *Aging Well: Surprising Guideposts to a Healthier Life*, psychiatrist Dr. George Vaillant details the results of his impressive 75-year study on adult development. One of his unexpected insights was that "participants who have aged most successfully worry less about cholesterol and waistlines and more about gratitude and forgiveness." Recent findings in the field of psychoneuroimmunology also indicate that emotions directly impact the body. Whereas negative emotions promote stress-related immune dysfunction and damage health, positive emotions promote health over the long term.

The recent Adverse Childhood Experiences (ACE) study found that childhood abuse and stress is held in the body, shortening life by as much as 20 years. Other studies have shown that positive mental health and stress management have genetically protective qualities, correlating with longer telomeres (the caps at the end of chromosomes), which in turn correlates with longer life. It seems that practicing gratitude and forgiveness can actually change one's biology. Heart rate variability—that is, the physiological process most reflective of the heart's physical health and physiological response to emotions—increases as we work through difficult emotions and situations. Rather than waiting for an anti-aging cure, aging adults can take matters into their own hands by beginning the hard work of healing toxic stress and cultivating positive experiences. Practiced over the long term, emotional health interventions such as counseling, support groups, meditation, and mindfulness can protect hearts and genes alike.

SIGNALS

#1

Crowdsourcing Mental Health

Co-founded in 2015 by technology design-ers Kareem Kouddous, Fraser Kelton, and Robert K. Morris, Koko is an app that allows users to crowdsource mental health advice. Users post about their troubles and stresses, and others weigh in with suggestions on how to rethink the problem. While cogni-tive behavioral therapy (CBT) is commonly used to reframe problems in clinical practice, and many apps connect users with mental health experts, Koko is one of just a hand-ful of apps that uses a peer-to-peer model to connect users to helpful advice from strang-ers. A limited study found that Koko boosts mental health, which isn't surprisingly given that its developers were informed by studies showing that CBT is as effective as prescrip-tion drugs for treating depression and anxi-ety, and that mental health improves when people have access to a safe space where they can share their feelings and experiences with supportive peers.

#2

Regulate Your Zs

The emergence of wearable technology, such as Apple Watches and Fitbits, has resulted in an increased awareness of how day-to-day habits affect health. One important habit is sleep and, more broadly, circadian rhythms. According to a Harvard Medical School arti-cle entitled "Sleep and Mental Health," sleep problems not only take an emotional toll—they also increase an individual's risk of devel-oping particular mental illnesses. Meanwhile, regulating sleep can help alleviate symptoms of some mental health problems. Similarly, *The Lancet Psychiatry* published a study looking at disruptions to circadian rhythms, defined as increased activity during the night, decreased activity during the day, or both. The study found that those who experienced more disruptions were more likely to have symp-toms of bipolar disorder or major depression, decreased feelings of well-being, and reduced cognitive functioning. Various technologies, such as Beddit, Basis, and SleepRate, have emerged to improve sleep patterns by offering a feedback loop on sleep activity.

"From a healthcare perspective, I think it's interesting that [HCPs are] so focused on making life [last] as long as possible, that they step off when it comes to death—not only as professionals, but as humans. I think that's a big opportunity for private companies to consider: How can we make a good death?"

Anne Danielsen, Senior
Service Designer, Dansk
Design Center, Excerpt
from Expert Interview

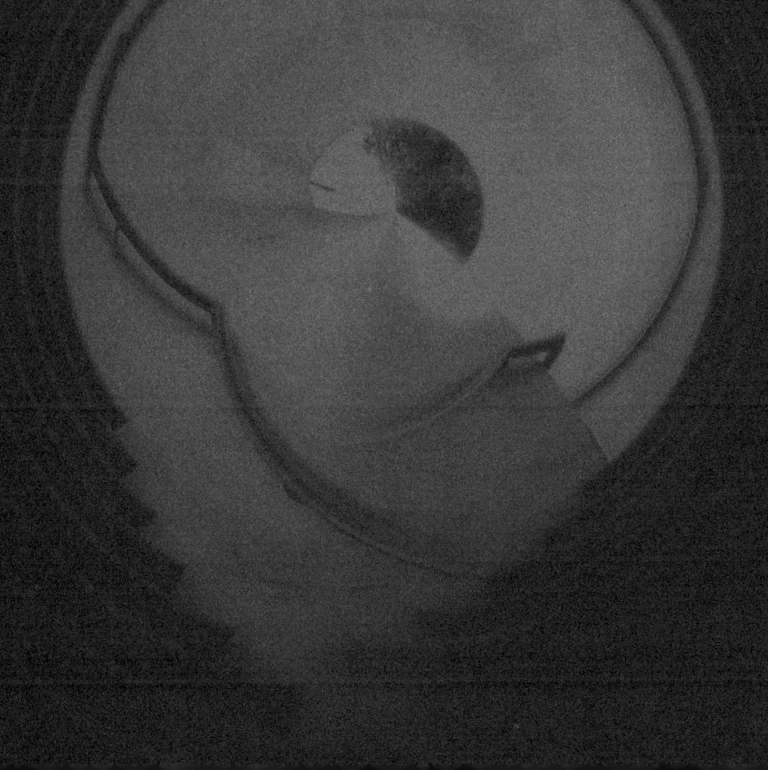

Bringing to Life the Future of Intervention

Building out possible concepts and solutions.

"...what care can mean in each situation cannot be resolved by ready-made explanations."

Maria Puig de la Bellacasa, Professor at the University of Leicester, "Matters of Care in Technoscience: Assembling Neglected Things," *Social Studies of Science*

Today, the traditional separation between mind and body is constantly being challenged, as is the dichotomy of environment and individual. As society evolves and science progresses, integrated approaches to healthcare will continue to grow in popularity. Still, the widespread acceptance of alternative healthcare interventions is likely a long way off; the adoption of a more integrative perspective on health will require continued proof and communication regarding the benefits of such an approach. This will be particularly true among seniors, many of whom will have already invested time and effort to become comfortable with how things were practiced in the past.

EXPERIENCE DRIVERS

Forces Influencing How Aging Adults Experience Intervention

To imagine how organizations can create more intelligent, human-centric services that address emergent shifts in health-care interventions for aging individuals, we must put the perspective of older adults at the forefront while also considering the continuously shifting perspectives that these individuals are inundated with on a regular basis. These perspectives often come from mainstream media, as well as from close friends and family members. The experience drivers below summarize key considerations and provide points of departure to keep in mind as we imagine ways to ease tensions and improve experiences for older adults.

1. Identity Politics

Negative stereotypes about how older adults think, act, and look prompt some to focus on finding ways to resist health-care interventions that affirm their elderly status.

> **How might we help seniors to embrace the realities of aging in a way that both appeals to and benefits them?**

2. Everyday Comforts

Whether through major lifestyle changes or daily physical and emotional difficulties, aging often brings unwelcome changes that drive many older adults to find comfort in the more consistent aspects of their lives.

> **How might we position healthy changes in ways that feel safe, yet compelling, to older adults?**

3. Emotional State

Pain can feel intensified when the recovery process is unknown and untested. This leads to serious physical, psychological, and emotional trauma, which can limit one's ability to think clearly and to feel capable of working through their recovery.

> **How might we help seniors heal emotionally?**

4. Lifestyle Choices

Seniors have spent a lifetime making decisions, and they may be protective of the choices they've made and routines they've developed.

> **How might we empower older adults to practice prevention as a part of their healthcare routine?**

OPPORTUNITY SPACE

Rethinking Health Interventions and Investing in the Right Initiatives

Given the systemic, experiential, and foresight perspectives brought forward, as well as the learnings we captured in our interviews with aging and healthcare experts across North America and Europe, we have defined an opportunity space as a takeaway for this chapter. We use opportunity spaces to capture the key thinking and findings uncovered in our research. These spaces are also intended to inform and inspire organizations across industries to design better futures, in this case, for older adults.

This chapter's opportunity space surrounding aging interventions intends to challenge conventional thinking around how people perceive and manage their health and wellness as they age.

Invest in Composition

Context

In a world that can feel fragmented and slow to translate new thinking into systemic change, individuals desire integrated interventions that address the depth and breadth of their health needs.

Opportunity Space

Explore opportunities that allow older adults to co-create their own health interventions and to compose individualized plans that enhance their well-being.

Staying healthy or becoming healthier is a multifaceted challenge that requires an understanding of how one's biological systems are affected by external factors. As advancements in biology and data science uncover interconnected mechanisms that impact each individual's health, holistic healthcare interventions will need to be formed based not only the underlying biological mechanisms of disease, but also on the lifestyle, emotional, and economic indicators tied to a person's health. Current health innovation processes must be adapted away from measurement-based models to ones that consider both biological and social outcome metrics. These new human-centric models of care would strike a better balance between overall population health and choices of older adults.

New opportunities are emerging within value-based models of care that aim to expand how people think about the quality of healthcare interventions. Yet, more still needs to be done to expand how we understand quality of care, as well as how we think about who and what matters when making decisions about the role of healthcare in someone's life. This is only possible if we continue to see health as part of a holistic experience of trying to live well in all aspects of life.

Reimagining Maria's Story

Throughout this chapter, we explored the current realities and challenges facing older adults in the context of healthcare interventions. We also traced some emerging trends and signals that are pushing us beyond the era of biomedicalization and toward a more holistic understanding of health, wellness, and aging.

In closing, we would like to reimagine Maria's story to explore some of the subtle ways in which her life could be improved if her own perspectives and ways of knowing herself were acknowledged, understood, and accepted by the people and institutions in her life. In this version of Maria's story, assumptions, beliefs, and attitudes about aging are not always explicitly discussed; however, they are enacted in Maria's interactions with her family. Such moments showcase the potential that a new model of aging would have to truly transform an individual's experience.

Maria couldn't help but smile as she flipped the last of the eggs. *Not a single broken yolk*, she thought to herself. It was a small but significant victory, one that wouldn't have been possible just last week.

For months, Maria had been working with her doctor to find a combination of medication that might reduce the tremor in her right hand. They had made some good progress, but the real success had been finding a new tool to help her in the kitchen. The special spatula, which her daughter Sofia had found online, was designed to stabilize the movement caused by a shaking hand. It took no time at all for her daughter to use the app to capture the specific dimensions and contours of Maria's hand. By answering a few short questions, Maria was able to articulate exactly how and where her discomfort manifested. It was the first time she felt like someone else really understood what she was experiencing when it came to living with Parkinson's on a daily basis. And, much to her family's amusement, Maria had been making breakfast for them every day for the past week.

Maria turned to face her other daughter, Cecilia, who was moving the plates Maria had prepared from the counter to the kitchen table. "Still smiling about that spatula, mama?" she teased. "I wish I could take the credit for that one. Who knew that eggs could make you so happy?"

"Not just any eggs," Maria laughed. "*Over easy* eggs! *Easy* being the key word!"

Maria turned off the stove before taking her spot at the table. Cecilia had placed Maria's medication, which was sorted into the correct doses in her new pill counter, next to her plate.

"Tony, you know that you're picking Abuela up from choir on your way home from soccer practice tonight, right?" Sofia asked.

Tony nodded as he chewed a bite of toast. "Got it," he said, his mouth still full.

"And Mama, you remember that Tina is picking you up on her way to the church, right?"

"Yes, Sofia, I remember."

Cecilia chimed in, grinning ear to ear. "You're not going to make poor Tina rescue you from that evil jacket again, are you?"

Maria tried to suppress a smile as her daughters and grandson all laughed, recalling her mishap from last week. When Tina had arrived to pick Maria up last Thursday, Maria was completely exasperated. She had been so focused on reading and learning the music for choir practice that she'd completely lost track of time. She had rushed to get her coat and shoes on; when Tina had opened the front door, there was Maria, sitting on the bench by the door with her right arm trapped in her jacket and her left shoe only halfway on her foot. Though she and Tina had laughed about the incident later, it was not something she was hoping to repeat any time soon.

"I will be at the door by 3:45, even if that means I have to start getting ready at noon," Maria replied dryly.

Later that day, Maria closed her eyes as she sang the songs she had worked so hard to learn the week before. Most of the choir stood, though a few older members, including Maria, sat comfortably in front of the others. The different voices of the choir came together, filling the church and sending chills down Maria's spine.

In that moment, she didn't worry about shaking, or losing her balance, or dropping anything. She didn't think about her medication, or about Tony picking her up soon. Her hearing troubles were of no concern here, either—the music was so loud and so clear that she could actually *feel* the sound in her chest. In that moment, Maria had a thought that made her smile: *I'm exactly where I'm meant to be.*

The Promise of Gerontechnology

SYSTEMIC

PERSPECTIVE

Disrupting Dependence

Understanding the current state.

"Technologies only come to life and have meaning as people use and adopt them. At the same time, technologies play a central role in the constitution of time regimes, as our very experience of human action and the material world is mediated by technology."

Judy Wajcman, Sociology Professor at LSE, from *Pressed for Time: The Acceleration of Life in Digital Capitalism*

People have long assumed that older adults cannot adapt to new technologies. This assumption is strongly tied to misinformed ideas about the physical and cognitive decline that occurs in old age, and to the perception that seniors are not interested in new experiences. While this generalization may have once been rooted in some truth, as technology has become more ubiquitous within society in general, so too has it been increasingly accepted by older adults. Today, many emerging technologies are giving this population new opportunities to achieve greater independence. Such innovations can improve people's lives across the different areas covered in this book: home and community (Chapter 1), health (Chapter 2), lifestyle and entertainment, continued education and employment, financial management (Chapter 4), and identity (Chapter 5). For older adults, the most significant area of impact of digital tools can be seen, perhaps, in the social effect of these technologies. According to a 2017 Pew Research Center survey, there has been an exponential rise in internet, social media, and smartphone usage by older adults in the US, with internet usage in particular seeing a significant increase from approximately 12% to 67% over the last two decades. The same survey found that over the past year, the adoption of voice-activated speakers has outpaced that of smartphones in the US, rising 78% from the previous year. This increase in usage by senior consumers may be attributed to the ease of use and multi-functionality of voice interface technologies.

Though aging adults are adopting technology at an impressive rate, new products created specifically for older adults are often designed with a strong emphasis on the perceived physical and cognitive decline of the intended users. As human–computer interaction researcher Amanda Lazar put it in an interview with *ScienceNode*, "Aging is often framed as a problem technology can solve, and older people are positioned as lonely and disengaged." Technology created with aging adults in mind include incontinence products, devices for blood sugar measurement, a wide variety of mobility aids, lift chairs, hearing aids, and pill cutters and dispensers, to name a few. Of course, many of these technologies can be useful and may even improve the quality of life for some seniors; however, it is problematic and inaccurate to assume that medical and mobility devices are the only technologies seniors can benefit from. By relying on the language of assistance and overemphasizing physical and cognitive deficits, the creators of these devices take agency away from their intended users—and, in the process, they reduce aging adults to little more than patients in decline. As Lazar reflects, "Research has largely devoted itself to compensate for perceived deficits rather than appeal to what older people actually want."

Gerontechnology

Researchers and developers are beginning to see a much broader range of opportunities for working with older adults to create technologies that meet their needs, desires, and experiences, including a richer appreciation for what it means to navigate the physical, emotional, and social dimensions of aging with agency. Gerontechnology is an entire field of research and design geared toward making technology specifically for older adults. The field has emerged as a result of two major 20th century trends that have only become more pronounced in the 21st. The first is the rapid proliferation of novel technological devices, platforms, and digital applications. The second is the steady increase in prominence of older segments of societies around the world. Gerontechnology marries engineering and science—like emerging developments in sensors, computation, and data science—with gerontology. Inherent to

the field is a desire to disprove and overcome assumptions about how older adults engage with technology. Gerontechnology recognizes that aging adults have the desire and ability to embrace a technological world—but they do not want such a world imposed on them. They want to be involved in its co-design, and they want services that they can actively manipulate to shape their personal experiences.

Advances in gerontechnology, and associated fields of research and innovation, do not just offer the possibility of improving the health of elderly users: They offer chances for increased social engagement and independent living throughout later life. As gerontechnology researcher Jeffrey Bardzell and his colleagues state in a paper for the CHI Conference on Human Factors in Computing Systems, aging is never just an era in which people need new devices only for the management of their health. Bardzell et al.

Gerontechnology recognizes that aging adults have the desire and ability to embrace a technological world—but they do not want such a world imposed on them.

suggest that menopause, for example, should be understood "as an era of life qualified not only by diverse physiological changes but also by changes in social, sexual, and even self-relations." This is just one of many examples of the novel frameworks emerging out of gerontechnology for tackling how best to address how older adults think about, engage, and ultimately work to help build new technologies that can help them age on their terms.

Key to gerontechnology's value is its emphasis on how the physical bodies, identities, and cognitive capacities of older adults shape and are shaped by novel technologies. For instance, gerontechnology more thoughtfully engages with questions of embodiment: that is, how older adults physically experience new devices, as well as how they engage with the digital worlds that such devices provide access to. This includes how the loss of vision, hearing, and

memories can offer new ways to incorporate everything from AI to specific physical design features to help people navigate daily life. Rather than focusing on a burden or a deficit, gerontechnology emphasizes the need to understand the contexts in which people experience changes in both a physical and cognitive capacity. For instance, gerontechnology has embraced broader debates in cognitive science around what researchers Raewyn Bassett and Janice E. Graham have described as dementia's ability to be "played out in the everyday world... as contextual, bounded, and interdependent states," not as a single process that needs to be reversed to improve someone's health.

At the same time, gerontechnology can help people avoid the pitfalls of what historians and sociologists of technology have called "technological determinism." Technological determinism is a way of thinking that assumes that technologies

used by a given society, in a particular time and place, independently shape the social, political, and cultural values of the people within that society, ultimately affecting how they understand the world. Technological determinism informs both utopian and dystopian visions of the future, visions that often fail to acknowledge the complex interactions between people and technology, and how these can be altered to better address particular needs and perspectives. With these challenges in mind, researchers in gerontechnology are calling for more inclusivity in the study and development of the field. This is, in part, to overcome the assumption that older adult users are all white, middle-class, and heterosexual.

Inclusive design is an important step toward allowing people to truly invest their own needs and desires into how they use particular devices and applications. As health sociologists Kelly Joyce, Meika Loe, and Lauren Diamond-Brown explain, "An examination of inequality, intersectionality, and gerontechnology is important for locating vectors of power in the process of technology creation, use, and meaning."

Guided by emerging questions, concerns, and developments in gerontechnology, this chapter explores how strategically equipping older adults with technology, and actively collaborating with them in the design of new technologies, can transform the experience of later life.

"We make a lot of assumptions about needs, and forget about people's wants and desires, and desires are critical to how we build new technologies for older adults. They need to drive the design."

Nicola Palmarini,
Researcher and
Entrepreneur at IBM,
Excerpt from Expert
Interview

The Role of Technology in Daily Life

Exploring the context of technological change.

"*The whole*, as modern science is insisting in many fields, is not merely the sum of all its parts, but the result of a unique arrangement and interrelation of the parts that has brought about a new entity. Gunpowder is not merely the sum of sulphur and charcoal and saltpeter, and no amount of knowledge even of all three of its elements in all the forms they take in the natural world will demonstrate the nature of gunpowder."

Ruth Benedict,
Anthropologist, from
Patterns of Culture

Older adults experience new technologies in a number of distinct ways, but there are two categories that stand out for the purposes of this book. In one case, aging adults are given new devices by family members, caregivers, or healthcare providers in the hopes that they will use the technology to overcome challenges associated with the physical and cognitive effects of aging. Devices created for this purpose are often designed with simple instructions, are more manual in nature, and provide a very narrow set of functions and features. In the second instance, older adults are introduced to, or feel a desire to engage with, smartphones, tablets, and a range of new features for "connected" and "smarter" living in the home. Over the last couple years, adoption of these latter technologies by seniors has grown, largely due to their ease of use.

There is, however, a disconnect between healthcare technologies and the broader world of connected, smart technology—what is often called the "internet of things," or, in the context of this book, the "internet of older things." That disconnect has to do with the lack of human and consumer-forward design thinking in healthcare technology, which has led to a lack of thoughtfully integrated healthcare devices within connected platforms used in other areas of daily life. In a recent interview with MobiHealth, Michael Dowling, CEO of Northwell Health, suggested that the key to overcoming this disconnect is a rephrasing of a core question: "It's not asking the question, 'What is the matter with you?' but 'What matters to you?'"

In this section, we explore the ways in which much of the technology designed for older adults is informed by a desire to solve for the burden of aging, rather than to challenge what aging is, how it should be experienced, and how it can be transformed in the near and distant future. What happens if, with the right sensitivity to the needs, desires, and experiences of older adults, healthcare innovations are integrated with the broader world of connected devices and digital environments to reshape what it means to age well?

Influence + Control

Though the technological landscape is shifting to better address their needs and experiences, many older adults still find that technologies are either imposed upon them, or make them feel alienated from the rest of the world. In the context of many healthcare devices, their value is defined and shaped by experts in medicine and information technology. This expertise is privileged over the bodily and emotional experiences of the people using these devices to navigate serious health concerns, as well as their loved ones. As outlined in the previous chapter, it is no longer helpful for experts to simply prescribe solutions: They must work collaboratively with patients and their loved ones to build more meaningful solutions for living well. This is especially important in the design of future healthcare technologies.

Because healthcare is so driven by outcomes, the design of these technologies tends to emphasize increased precision, accuracy, and efficiency of information. The actual experience of using these devices—whether one is bringing them into the home or using them in external spaces—is completely left out of the actual design process. People with chronic conditions often find, for instance, that they fear traveling because of the bulky and cumbersome nature of technologies designed solely for the purpose of dealing with a specific health issue. This, of course, unfolds to the detriment of people's lived experiences, and to the emotional and social complexities that shape what living with various health and wellness issues looks and feels like.

On the other hand, more consumer-focused smart, mobile, and connected devices—including those designed by technology giants like Apple and Google—also ignore the experiences and needs of older adults, though in a slightly different way. While healthcare devices are narrow in scope, consumer goods are more universal, with the assumption being that they can become embedded in the lives of everyone. Smartphones, tablets, and connected home applications have mostly been designed with and for a younger segment of the population; the willingness of older adults to adapt to new technologies, on the other hand, is tied to a unique set of considerations, needs, desires, and capabilities.

In an article for *Frontiers in Psychology*, authors Vaportzis, Clausen, and Gow argue that aging adults have a values-based approach to adopting new technologies, which contributes to their slower rates of adoption. They do not share a younger person's desire to keep up with trends, which

Older adults often worry about the extent
to which new devices, platforms, and
applications can help them in maintaining
their quality of life. Defining what quality of
life means for them and them alone is key.

has led many companies to the assumption
that they cannot adapt. However, they are
far more engaged than expected, as older
adults often worry about the extent to which
new devices, platforms, and applications can
help them in maintaining their quality of life.
Defining what quality of life means for them
and them alone is key. This group will often
reject technologies made without their values
in mind.

This is not to say that every older adult
needs specially designed devices; rather, the
richness and complexity of aging requires
technology that is adaptable to a variety of
bodies, experiences, and capabilities. Aging
adults tend to lack influence or control
over the design trajectory of new technologies, including devices specifically made for
their health and wellness needs and those
designed for their hobbies, social and political engagement, entertainment, etc.

"**Technology, as such, makes nothing happen. By now, however, the
concept has been endowed with a
thing-like autonomy and a seemingly magical power of historical
agency.**"

Leo Marx, Historian of Technology,
"Technology: The Emergence of a
Hazardous Concept,"
Technology and Culture

Assistance +
Independence

Assistive technologies are defined in a number of ways, but at their core they are devices, platforms, and applications that improve people's ability to function in daily life. Government programs, like Ontario's Assistive Devices Program, define a range of technologies as assistive, in categories as diverse as mobility aids, hearing devices, visual aids, diabetes equipment, respiratory tools, facial and limb prosthetics, orthotics, enteral-feeding supplies, and more. This category can also include AI-driven sensors that allow people to easily monitor friends and loved ones who wish to live on their own, but need immediate help when trouble arises. It is no surprise that assistive technologies are critical for improving the lives of many aging adults.

However, assistive technologies are not always designed with the holistic experiences of older adults in mind, leading to barriers in adoption. Many older adults feel

both unaware and uninformed about what assistive technologies are available to them, while others become frustrated by the learning curve for using a device, knowing who to contact when the device breaks down, or the incompatibility of some devices with their homes or daily routines. Because these devices are often made to overcome a single physiological limitation in someone's health, assistive technologies are judged only by the extent to which they do that one job well—a judgement often made without the user's perspective in mind. This limits the extent to which the needs, desires, and preferences of older adults and their loved ones are being addressed in the design of these devices, and it also impacts the access users have to this technology.

There is a need for assistive technologies to be more thoughtfully embedded into users' daily lives. This includes a need for different assistive devices to easily

To truly make people independent, the
idea of assistance has to be broadened
to something beyond overcoming a
single physiological impairment.

communicate with one another. People
often get frustrated when the use of certain
assistive technologies for chronic conditions, such as respiratory conditions, forces
them to stay home from a social gathering or long trip, simply because they were
not designed to be used on the move.
Unfortunately, there are limits to the extent
that the rest of the world can currently
accommodate assistive technologies. People
become frustrated by inaccessible roads,
sidewalks, restaurants, community centers,

and public spaces of all kinds. They want
the world to recognize the value of accom-
modating and adapting to the needs of
older adults, especially those living with
serious disabilities and chronic conditions,
so that they may fully enjoy the world
around them.

Caregivers and loved ones also suffer
through the challenge of inadequate access
to assistive technologies. To truly make
people independent, the idea of assistance
has to be broadened to something beyond

overcoming a single physiological impairment. The limits of assistive devices present as much of a challenge for designing technology as they do for designing the environments in which older people—especially those with chronic diseases and disabilities—live, work, and play on a daily basis.

"It is becoming gradually evident that the assistance needs for older adults have to rely upon automatization technologies to assist traditional human caregivers. These emerging widespread technologies available in 'Smart Homes' can in fact enable less differentiated caregivers to provide assisted help. Hetero caregivers (formal and informal), if supported by technology, can deliver better assistance if duly directed by evidence-based AI tooling."

Césa Fonseca, David Mendes, Manuel Lopes, Artur Romão, and Pedro Parreira, "Deep Learning and IoT to Assist Multimorbidity Home Based Healthcare," *Journal of Medical and Health Informatics*

Security +

Privacy

Older adults have complicated experiences with issues of security and privacy when using connected devices, platforms, and applications. They are more likely to proactively put passwords and other security measures on their computers, phones, homes, and other physical and digital devices, platforms, and applications. Yet, conversations around security and privacy in technology often fail to account for the complex experiences of older adults. Discourse around these topics tends to come from a view where older adults are victims of security breaches, rather than active agents capable of navigating these issues on their own terms. Ultimately, security and privacy do not feel like issues that can be handled by older adults, but instead problems that need to be solved by security experts and the more technologically-savvy people in older adults' lives.

In a paper for the journal *Gerontechnology*, Linda Boise and colleagues found that the adoption of at-home

Older adults and caregivers want some autonomy and visibility with regards to the management of their data, especially if, in the future, the sources of data are their home appliances, furniture, and even the sheets on their beds.

monitoring technology indicated that older
adults are receptive to having an additional
set of "digital eyes" on them when choosing
to age in place. While many older adults are
reluctant to share their data, and additionally express that they want to manage their
daily affairs on their own, they also acknowledge that severe illness can arise without
warning and cause them to become more
vulnerable when living alone. The fear of
not being able to readily obtain help in an
emergency may supercede concerns over
privacy.

Boise and her team also found that the
willingness to share personal health information is influenced by whom older adults
will be sharing this with, the authority that
they will have in providing information, and
the implicit and explicit intentions of how
their data will be used. In other words, older
adults and caregivers want some autonomy
and visibility with regards to the management of their data, especially if, in the future,
the sources of data are their home appliances, furniture, and even the sheets on
their beds.

**"The first step in protecting and
controlling access to data is to
find it, but by no means is this an
easy problem to solve. Think of
all the variations on basic account
numbers, let alone more complex
internet-era patterns. Developing
algorithms to match these
patterns will require more than
an ad-hoc solution."**

Yaki Faitelson, "Data Privacy
Disruption in the US," *Forbes*

Lam Wei's Story

Bringing to life current challenges in technology use for independent living.

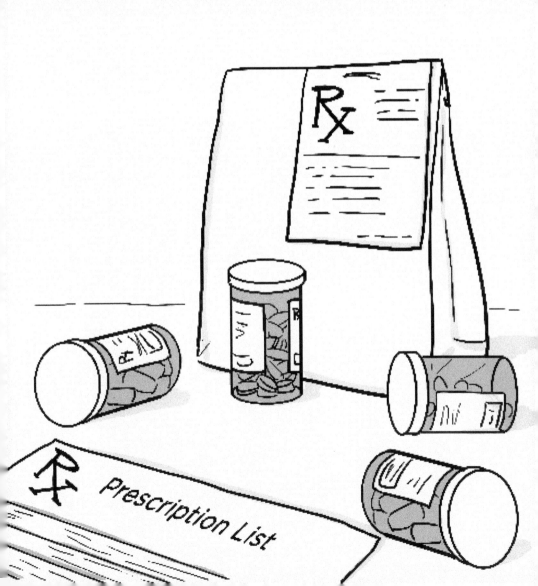

To help bring to life the concepts explored throughout this book, we have created personas for each chapter. A persona grounds ethnographic research within an individual narrative and reveals how overarching themes may play out for a particular person.

The persona for this chapter is Lam Wei, whose story is intended to bring to life insights about how older adults interact with technology. Here, we look at how the challenges discussed so far may manifest in Lam Wei's life. At the end of the chapter, we will see another version of Lam Wei's story: one in which Lam Wei's use of technology enables her to maintain the independent lifestyle she longs for, while also supporting her safety and wellness.

Lam Wei is in her late seventies. She lives in her own apartment in a seniors' apartment, but she still works part-time at a nearby café. Although she suffers from arthritis and diabetes, Lam Wei is still very active and doesn't do well with a sedentary lifestyle. She spent most of her life running her family's local grocery store, and rarely took a full weekend off. Her daughter, Nikki, visits regularly, but she often expresses concern that Lam Wei is spending too much time busy-bodying. She worries that her mother doesn't take care of herself properly, particularly when it comes to taking her medication.

The story below represents a brief glimpse into Lam Wei' daily life, including the challenges she faces around retaining her independence while giving her family peace of mind.

Lam Wei drained the last of the jasmine tea her daughter, Nikki, dropped off yesterday. She wolfed down a steamed bun and quickly cleaned up the kitchen—she hated leaving dishes in the sink—all the while grimacing through the throbbing in her fingers. She had remembered her arthritis medication that morning, if only because the pain was worse when she woke up and incredibly distracting. The medication still hadn't kicked in yet.

She showered and dressed quickly. She had slept in too late and had to get to the café for her shift, which began at 10. She hated being late; she had never been late opening the shop that Nikki now ran—not once in 50 years.

There was a knock at the door. "Lam Wei?" It must have been Arjun, she thought, a member of the home-care service that Nikki had insisted Lam Wei sign up for. The home-care team checked in on Lam Wei regularly to make sure she was taking her medication, and to remind her of upcoming appointments.

She opened the door for him, then went back to putting on jewelry—final touches were always important.

"Are you getting ready for work?" Arjun asked with a smile. Though she knew he meant well, Lam Wei always found Arjun slightly condescending, as if he found it adorable that a small and seemingly frail woman like Lam Wei still had a job.

"I know you're taking a shift at the café this morning, so I wanted to speak with you before you left," he said, then held up a white paper bag. "This is the modified medication regimen your doctor prescribed yesterday."

"Thank you, Arjun, but I really need to leave," Lam Wei said.

"This will only take a minute. It's important that we do this."

"I'll give you five minutes. I'm watching the clock."

Arjun laughed, but Lam Wei was serious. She planned to cut him off the second his time was up.

They sat in the kitchen as Arjun quickly ran through the bottles and multi-colored pills. Though she nodded along, Lam Wei was more focused on the clock than on the instructions.

"Do you have any questions?" Arjun asked. Lam Wei shook her head. "Good. I'll be back in a few days to see how it's going. I'll send an update to Nikki as well. She'll want to know what you're on."

Of course she would. Lam Wei didn't even try to fight the updates anymore; Nikki was paying half the bill, after all. And although Lam Wei would never admit it, it was a bit of a relief to know she could ask Nikki for clarification, should she forget which pills she was supposed to take with food.

After a quick goodbye, Arjun slipped out the door and Lam Wei put the final touches on her hair. She struggled to get her coat on, her fingers still throbbing. She felt like she was forgetting something, but she had just enough time to make it to work if she speed-walked. *That will be fun for my knees*, she thought.

Lam Wei made it to the café with less than a minute to spare. She still had a nagging feeling that she had forgotten something, but she set herself up at the cashless till instead. It had been a challenge at first, but she was getting the hang of this tablet thing pretty well now.

Her phone buzzed in her pocket, but she ignored it while she served customers. It buzzed again, then again, then once more. She didn't have to look to know it was Nikki. She waited until her break; making her daughter wait gave her a strange sense of gleeful satisfaction. She loved Nikki, of course, but she didn't enjoy the constant check-ins. She was perfectly capable of taking care of herself.

Lam Wei went into the break room to check her messages. Most of Nikki's voice and text messages were asking if she was feeling okay, if she needed any cooked meals, if she'd taken both her arthritis and her diabetes medi—

Oh.

Lam Wei's shoulders dropped. That's what had been nagging at her—the diabetes medication. She would have to extend her break and go back home to take it. Her manager would be understanding, she knew that. Still, she hated having to ask. It was so unprofessional.

FORESIGHT
SHIFTS

Transforming How We Leverage Technological Change

The power of gerontechnology.

"Older adults' perceptions and use of technology are embedded in their personal, social, and physical context. Awareness of these psychological and contextual factors is needed in order to facilitate aging in place through the use of technology."

Sebastiaan Peek,
Behavioral Scientist,
"Older Adults' Reasons
for Using Technology
While Aging in Place,"
Gerontology

To understand how the aging population will come to redefine technology, we must first identify and articulate "shifts"—that is, large-scale transitions that are taking place within society today. We use these shifts to help articulate the tensions that emerged during the foresight research phase of this book, which involved diverse scanning of various moments of change influencing Western society, whether that comes in the form of a film, article, tech startup, or conversation. Shifts allow us to frame new questions and establish future-oriented points of view, enabling us to imagine and create more meaningful realities for aging individuals.

SHIFT 1

From Institutional Aging

to Living in Place

Many aging individuals want to live independently in their own homes with access to local services for as long as possible. Smarthomes and digital assistants may help meet the health needs of the elderly so that they can successfully live in place.

"A home isn't a medical facility; it's a domestic space. And when we're developing products and technology for aging in place, we can't lose sight of the fact there's a level of dignity that people shouldn't have to give up in old age."

John Brown, Dean of the University of Calgary's Faculty of Environmental Design, Excerpt from interview with *The Globe and Mail*

> The Choice to Stay Home

Older adults today are increasingly reluctant to forfeit their independence and leave the comfort of their own homes to move into institutions, but until recently, few alternatives existed for those in need of long-term assistance and care. A greater range of less-expensive living (and care) options are needed for those who are too healthy to be occupying a bed in an institution, but too sick or frail (and lacking in available support) to remain in their place of choice: their home. Providing older adults with more options for living in place would help ease the pressure placed on both institutions and individuals (mostly friends and family) providing care and places of residence. Key to solving this problem may be the emergence of smart-homes that incorporate various technologies to minimize risks and support older adults' health and independence.

66

'"When you ask most people where they want to die,' Volandes said—referring, of course, to people who have some context for the nature of the question—'most people say, I want to die outside of the hospital, in my home, in comfort.'

Nearly 80 percent of Americans, in fact, say that. And yet, close to 55 percent of older adults die in a hospital or nursing home. Fewer than one in four manage to die at home. Why does this discrepancy persist?"

James Hamblin, MD, "The Fallacy of 'Giving Up,'" *The Atlantic*

From Obligatory Moves to Exercising Choice

The integration of monitoring and assistive technologies into the home promises to help those with mobility and cognitive challenges achieve autonomy and minimize risk. Increasingly, devices make it possible to adapt or redesign existing homes using wearables, webcams, digital assistants, and medical and activity sensors. Robotic machines that can replicate the services of remote healthcare providers using visual sensors and physical effectuators are now a reality. Devices can monitor the activities of daily living, such as sleep, heart rate, blood pressure, and gait and movement. They alert family and healthcare providers of distress, a change in health status, a fall, or if the patient has forgotten to take their medication. Smart devices turn off the stove if it has accidentally been left on, refrigerators monitor eating habits, and floors detect changes in weight. Sleep sensors, gait analysis, and smart screens send automated reminders to patients for daily tasks.

As well as supporting independence at home and helping to reduce worry and anxiety for families, connecting older adults with healthcare systems helps to prevent unnecessary hospital admissions and allows

Older adults should still control what is monitored, when it is monitored, and by whom.

for earlier discharge. These systems allow clinicians to diagnose, manage, and monitor patients in their homes remotely, saving the healthcare system money, and reducing trips to the clinic or hospital for patients. Most importantly, when AI is built into these new technologies, they can predict changes in normal behavior before they even happen, enabling proactive intervention.

While connected homes offer benefits that include increased independence for older adults and decreased costs for healthcare systems, it is important that new monitoring systems and digital surveillance not interfere with an individual's ability to live their life. Older adults often feel as if they give up their independence when they enter a hospital, long-term care facility, or

a loved one's home. Technologies that turn the home into a virtual institution will make many older adults uncomfortable as well. Feeling spied on in the privacy of their own homes—even if only by their families and members of their care team—may be hard for many to accept.

The challenge going forward will be to design gerontechnology systems that allow for integrated, cost-efficient assistive and monitoring systems that provide peace of mind for the individual's family while also respecting their need for privacy and independence. Such systems would make older adults feel cared for, rather than interfered with. One size will not fit all, however. Older adults should still control what is monitored, when it is monitored, and by whom. It is also essential that this technology works as it should. If a family member relies on monitoring technologies to report issues in the home of an aging parent, and a signal is lost, data not uploaded, or any other issue arises, the consequences could be very serious.

SIGNALS

#1

Connected Living, Independently

Unlike the wearables that are increasingly being developed to monitor specific biomedical vitals, home sensor systems such as SmartThings or TruSense promise to bring peace of mind to people, their families, and their caregivers by monitoring older adults in their homes in a more subtle way. Whereas wearables can be bulky and awkward, and cameras feel invasive as they capture and record every movement, systems of seamless, smart sensors can be placed strategically around the house to ambiently track motions and activities, generating alerts only when there are inconsistencies in the data detected. If a change in habits occurs, these sensors respond by doing things like turning on lights when inhabitants enter a room or step out of bed, turning off the stove if it's left on, or sending an alert if one's parent fails to appear in the kitchen at their usual time in the morning, for example.

Everyone from *Forbes* to analysts at the *Aging in Place Technology Watch* call out the increasing importance of voice-first technologies, especially voice-enabled home speakers from Google and Amazon. With these technologies, it will be increasingly possible for older people to live independent lives, unencumbered by bulky wearables or interfaces and design features that often take too long to learn.

#2

Proactive and Predictive Living

The less intrusive, more comprehensive, and more connected a system of sensors, the more useful it is, and the greater the chance it will be adopted. Medical sensors are no exception. Heart rate, blood pressure, glucose and oxygen levels, body temperature, hydration levels, and urine output are physiological parameters that can now be measured using sensor-based home health monitoring devices. By relaying data back to healthcare providers, these systems gather data to inform treatment decisions in real time. The hope is that they will soon make it possible to identify warning signals and risk factors in order to intervene proactively, thereby eliminating the need for hospitalization. The healthcare system will need to develop more integrative service models that can easily adapt to new personalized healthcare technologies. This should include systems that allow people in major healthcare facilities to respond quickly to information; the systems should also provide access to the tools that healthcare workers need to determine their engagement with patients.

"...we're taking a holistic approach to prevention, so we're combining sensory cognitive training, mindfulness, social interaction, nutrition, exercise, and emotional well-being, and looking at the interaction among these different factors. With clinical trials, we're told, 'Pick one variable that is most important.' But now we can use AI and machine learning for data analysis to see how many factors are interacting, and I think this is where we're going to have the biggest impact."

Allison Sekular, Vice-President of Research at Baycrest; Sandra A. Rotman Chair in Cognitive Neuroscience; and Managing Director of the Centre for Aging + Brain Health Innovation (CABHI) at the Rotman Research Institute, Excerpt from Expert Interview

SHIFT 2

From Limitless Life Spans

to Increased Health Spans

While immortality has always loomed as a possibility, never before has it been a more realistic pursuit. As we explore new means through which we can extend life (both biologically and digitally), we are being forced to confront questions about what it means to be human and who (if anyone) has the right to extend life forever.

"The healthcare system is doing a good job of helping people live longer and stronger lives, but aging is still a terminal condition [...] I believe it's inevitable we're going to solve aging at some point."

Joon Yun, Founder of the Race Against Time Foundation, Excerpt from interview with *Medium*

Disarming Time

People are used to utopian stories about how emerging technologies will deliver on the promise of limitless life and immortality. Whether it's changing human biology to live longer or changing notions of self and life in the pursuit of digital immortality, these technologies are challenging our notions of what it means to be human. However, not everyone is inspired by technological visions of the future where, free of our bodies, we can live on in digital form. Many are instead opting to focus on technological solutions that promise to maximize the years of life we already have.

66

"As we reflect on the relation between time and experience, for instance, there is an interesting and important paradox to be observed: the more life is experienced as meaningful, the less we are aware of time. [...] In those activities that constitute human happiness there seem to be no time and space, no subject and object. From this one may infer that what we basically seek as human beings is not more time to live, but meaningful experiences."

Martien Pijnenburg, Radboud University, and Carlo Leget, University of Humanistic Studies, "Who Wants to Live Forever? Three Arguments Against Extending the Human Lifespan," *Journal of Medical Ethics*

> Matching Healthspan to Lifespan

Science is pushing us to rethink who we are, how we engage each other, and how new technologies will alter how we understand the unfolding of our lives. Futurist Ray Kurzweil believes humans are now in the state of "longevity escape velocity," which means that for every year we are alive, our life expectancy is being extended by just over one year. Life extension and "permanent virtual retirement" may one day become a reality—although only for those who can afford it. Rather than being seduced and distracted by the promise of living forever, however, most major health and wellness initiatives focus on enabling more years spent in good health. While some technology innovators indulge in visions of longevity and devote infinite resources toward extending the human lifespan, the health and wellness industries remain committed to finding ways to avoid, manage, or treat ailments that currently prevent many from living well longer.

Health-adjusted life expectancy (HALE) is a measure developed by the WHO to assess the quality of health throughout people's lives. A person's HALE represents the average number of years they might expect to be in "full health" compared to years spent contending with injury, disease, and other circumstances. Measuring healthspan separately from lifespan is important, in part because it allows for a more personalized understanding of where an individual fits within population-level increases in life expectancy. One significant area of development here is

To think in terms of healthspans is to consider the richer social, cultural, environmental, and financial contexts that impact how people navigate their health and wellness.

pharmacogenomics, a field that studies how genes impact an individual's response to specific drugs. Researchers in this field are developing more robust tests for helping people see how their reactions will change over time. This will help people better understand how to alter treatments as they age, and it will also help patients work with their doctors to better assess the potential benefits of new drugs as they come to market.

Healthspans are about so much more than personalized and precision medicine; they go far beyond the molecular and genetic aspects of an older person's body. To think in terms of healthspans is to consider the richer social, cultural, environmental, and financial contexts that impact how people navigate their health and wellness. It is about designing better physical and digital environments for people to navigate their physical and cognitive health, while also looking at the ways in which social interaction, money, and education all play unique roles in helping people live longer, healthier, and more meaningful lives.

SIGNALS

#1

Immersive Therapeutics

Innovative technologies are creating new platforms to deliver therapies that improve health. For example, recent studies suggest that the sense of immersion created by virtual reality helps to combat pain, reducing everything from joint pain to cancer pain, as it tricks the user's cortical sensors into thinking that the computer-generated environment is real. With the aim of producing the right virtual experience for each person based on their needs and interests, AppliedVR in California has already designed 24 worlds that are meant to help those who wear their glasses to relax, escape, or become distracted. In Vancouver, the digital therapeutics company Mindful Garden has built a platform to help reduce anxiety, agitation, and aggression in hospitalized patients experiencing delirium and dementia. For example, an interactive garden experience facilitated via computer-generated imagery might be triggered in response to agitated movements and sounds detected via biosensor input (heart rate, galvanic response, respiratory rate, etc.).

#2

New Financing Vehicles to Increase Health

There is a paradox of financing for health: over 90% of what causes poor health has nothing to do with formal healthcare that one receives, yet over 90% of health resources are used in formal medical care. Shifting healthcare budgets from "sick care" toward prevention will likely be a task for the future; for now, novel financing vehicles for "health creation" are emerging. For example, looking to prevent heart disease and stroke, the Canadian Heart & Stroke Foundation's new Community Hypertension Prevention Initiative (CHPI) has created a Social Impact Bond funding model. This model uses performance-based contracts between private investors who put up capital (on risk) and public service agencies who deliver social programs. Investors are only repaid (in this case by the Public Health Agency of Canada) as specified goals and outcomes are reached. Funding for the CHPI was organized by the MaRS Centre for Impact Investing. They found private investors to fund programs that will be delivered by the Heart & Stroke Foundation in partnership with the YMCA and Shoppers Drug Mart, a major Canadian retail pharmacy chain. The program targets older adults at risk of developing hypertension and helps them adopt healthier habits. With $4 million at stake, it is hoped that the program will deliver on targets for patient participation and blood pressure levels.

SHIFT 3

From Biologically-Determined Life Stages

In an age-fluid world enabled by medical and reproductive technologies, life decisions will no longer be dictated by biology—meaning we may soon be able to do what we want, whenever we want.

"Youth's like diamonds in the sun, and diamonds are forever. Do you really want to live forever?"

Alphaville, from the song "Forever Young"

to Tech-Enabled Age Fluidity

Forever Young

"A zoomer has the body of a 65 year old, the mind of a 45 year old, the libido of a 25 year old, and the heart of a teenager," according to media visionary Moses Znaimer. In other words, a "zoomer" (defined as "a boomer with zip" by the Canadian lifestyle magazine of the same name) is someone who feels younger than their age. Today, being in the body of a 65 year old often still entails suffering the stigma of ageism, or the aches and pains of age-related conditions—but could this stereotype be changing? Researchers, like João Pedro de Magalhães of the University of Liverpool, are developing genomic technologies that combine cutting-edge biological research with powerful new software. These advances are changing the foundations on which we understand aging, resulting in new approaches that may lead to greater preservation of health in later years. At the same time, a greater sensitivity to the vibrancy of what it means to age well is leading older people to be generally more active than the elderly of generations past. We increasingly talk about an ageless future, where our years no longer define our identity. Could we be on a trajectory to living youthfully forever?

"Death organizes our lives. Because we have a finite end, we have a timeline for ourselves: when to settle down, when to have kids, when to let go. As humans, we make choices based on opportunity costs, which are priced in the currency of time—our most precious resource."

Dr. Ian Ground, philosopher at the University of Newcastle, Excerpt from a debate hosted by Intelligence Squared

> Life Stages Become Customizable, Not Predetermined

Today, we largely organize our lives around biological life stages, up to and including death. This only adds to the problem, as described earlier, that aging is often experienced as a limiting factor associated with various degrees of cognitive and/or physical decline. This explains why people hope that biotechnologies will add more good years to their lives, making them ageless by fulfilling their wish to remain vigorous and healthy until the end. Many people today experience adulthood as a time of proactive decision making, during which they plan (and save for) the big milestones in life, such as their career, marriage, parenthood, and retirement. In the future, people will increasingly be able to feel and behave younger for much longer.

With the help of reproductive technologies, women can now delay having children until well into their forties and beyond; as technology improves and becomes more accessible, egg freezing, IVF, and artificial-womb technologies could remove most age-related barriers to

reproduction. Yet, we still live in a world where women over 35 are described as having geriatric pregnancies. In the future, as we increasingly replace or augment parts of our aging bodies, it will become more difficult for society to presume that advancing age makes someone unfit to remain in the workplace, or to believe that they lack what it takes to become a student again. Having overcome the limitations of the aging body, the university of the future will serve those aged 18–80+, people will have the option of working into their nineties, and to have babies whenever they (finally) decide to. With a large percentage of the world's wealth concentrated in aging populations, we'll likely see interest in anti-aging technologies increase.

SIGNALS

#1

Virtual Memory, Virtual Tourism

Virtual technologies can create dynamic new pathways for people with memory loss to recall events and remain more active in many aspects of life. University of Pennsylvania psychologist Michael Kahana has led research that illustrates how algorithms in machine learning might be used to actively trigger people's memories. As fellow psychologist Youssef Ezzyat and his colleagues explain, "We apply targeted stimulation to the lateral temporal cortex and report that this stimulation rescues periods of poor memory encoding. This system also improves later recall, revealing that the lateral temporal cortex is a reliable target for memory enhancement."

There are also major developments in reminiscence therapy. This area of focus has had a powerful impact on dementia care, and it is now being embedded in the design of new VR tools to add an immersive dimension to the field. Virtue Health's LookBack headset, for instance, has a set of features that allow patients to look at different locations that speak to particularly important moments in their lives. Results from this kind of work open new possibilities that go beyond helping dementia sufferers recall memories, to allowing people to recall other kinds of information so that they can remain active and productive beyond the context of healthcare.

#2

Calibrating Age

As life expectancy increases and people become healthier, some are arguing that it no longer makes sense to categorize people as "old" based on how long they've lived, but that we should instead consider "prospective age"—that is, how much longer the individual has to live. For example, we could measure an individual's health and productivity levels and classify them as "old" once they have, on average, 15 years left to live. Dutch pensioner Emile Ratelband is one

person challenging how people are categorized by age. Although he's 69 years old, he says he can physically function as if he's in his forties and argues that a younger birth year would improve his life. He believes that not only would his prospects on Tinder improve, but that he would also be a more successful life coach, as people would be less likely to question his ability to relate to younger clients. He believes that the law should acknowledge his individual biological age rather than the date on his birth certificate. Although the court denied his initial appeal to get the year on his certificate changed to 20 years earlier, Ratelband continues to argue that if we can change our name or gender, we should also be able to change our age.

SHIFT 4

From Human Replacement

to Human Augmentation

People tend to think of personal and home-based technological devices as augmenting and empowering human capacity, while robots and units of AI replace their mental and physical work. This can sometimes feel isolating, as though it's impossible to be productive while also meeting one's human needs. However, this need not be the case. A new perspective on the collaborative and empowering potential of intelligent technologies could be all that's needed to reshape what it means to live and age well.

66

"Control leads to compliance, autonomy leads to engagement."

Daniel H. Pink, Author, from
Drive: The Surprising Truth About What Motivates Us

> Building Humanity Into Intelligent Technology

Numerous careers in science fiction writing and filmmaking have been built on the image of a dystopian future in which AI takes over everyday life, replacing people with robots and destroying all aspects of human experience. And yet, many of the most popular advances in technology over the course of the past several decades are hardly making humans obsolete. Rather, they require and even thrive on human intervention in order to function well. Fear of becoming a cyborg is being replaced with a recognition that smart technologies can be collaborative. This type of technology empowers people to remain active and engaged with their loved ones and to continue being professionally productive well into older age. Beyond the cyborg is a future where humans recognize the role they can play in shaping technologies, a future where devices, platforms, and applications are embedded in sincerely human modes of experience.

In this future, the world will be different—but it does not have to be unrecognizable. People can and should strive for a future in which AI, robots, and genetic therapies are geared toward foundational human needs for purpose, love and companionship, intimacy, and productivity. This could be the reward for a more thoughtful engagement with technology that connects novel innovations to our morals, ethics, as well as personal and social identities.

"If we wish to build not only better machines, but better relationships with and through machines, we need to start talking far more richly about the qualities of these relationships; how precisely our thoughts and feelings and biases operate; and what it means to aim beyond efficiency at lives worth living."

Tom Chatfield, Broadcaster and Philosopher, from "What Does It Mean to Be Human in the Age of Technology?," *The Guardian*

Human *with* (not *or*) Machine

Older adults today have adapted to a variety of technologies. They have learned to use various devices, platforms, and applications to help them in daily life. Increasingly, people talk about the power of devices, programs, and machines to augment and modify the work that many people want to continue doing well into their old age. Going forward, people will look for integrative qualities in their devices that are powerful, but also more subtle and embedded. This will include modifications to their own minds and bodies that help them feel as though they are still engaging in the human activities they have long valued. In short, gardeners will still want to garden, runners will still want to run, and painters will still want to paint—they just may need a new kind of assistance to do so.

The possibilities are less important than giving older adults the ability to customize how, if at all, they choose to augment or modify their physical and cognitive selves. For example, older people may want prosthetics that engage more directly with their central nervous systems; they may desire strong, data-driven exoskeletons to support their increasingly frail muscles; or they may even look to sensors to help their hands, ears, eyes, and feet navigate the world around them. They may turn to AI to help them predict health issues before they happen, or they may come to rely on AR and VR to manage pain. Regardless of the technology, there will need to be cultural shifts in how we understand the relationships between humans and the machines that they depend on; otherwise, novel forms of discrimination may bubble to the surface. More importantly, individuals can and should determine the extent to which they incorporate these innovations into their lives. A shift toward increasingly hybrid bodies could blur the boundary between people and the devices, platforms, and applications they build. The cultural and ethical issues relevant to such technological innovations are vast, but if this technology is designed with care and attention, it could benefit older adults considerably.

SIGNALS

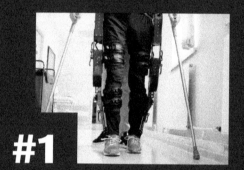

#1

Hybrid Bodies

Panasonic, Hyundai, Samsung and many emerging health tech startups are developing robotic exoskeletons to augment and extend the strength of adults working in many different industries. Originally developed to support the rehab of wounded veterans in the US, these supportive exoskeleton suits can also be used to increase the strength of those working in nursing care, or to increase mobility and self-reliance among the elderly. While initial models were bulky and slow, newer versions are soft and can be worn next to the body, like clothing. Rather than providing continuous assistance, newer models can be activated as needed, collaborating with, rather than controlling, a person's movements. One version of the suit, the Active Pelvis Orthosis, consists of a waist brace that is connected via carbon-fiber motor links to thigh braces. Worn by someone who is at risk for falling, this device senses when a person's legs diverge from a natural gait in a way that suggests a slip. It then applies force to support the legs, thereby helping to counteract a fall. On a smaller scale, the Stediglove by Revera helps those with Parkinson's steady their hand movements, making it easier to eat, get dressed, and perform other activities that require fine motor skills.

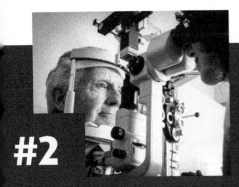

#2

Sensory Aid

The loss of hearing and eyesight can significantly impact an individual's health as they age, leading to social isolation and decreased cognition. While laser surgery can sometimes limit the extent of deteriorating eyesight, a new non-surgical option is now available for those with failing eyesight caused by macular degeneration—a medical condition common in older adults, in which a person experiences blurred or reduced vision in the center of their visual field. While most people tend to associate VR with enhanced entertainment, the company IrisVision has developed a VR application to be used as therapy for those with macular degeneration. IrisVision's smartphone-based VR system helps people to see better by recording a person's surroundings, and then magnifying and displaying it in real time in a person's periphery, where they still have vision. This technology is already being used in 80 ophthalmology centers in the US.

Bringing to Life the Future of Gerontechnology

Building out possible concepts and solutions.

"Good design is obvious.
Great design is invisible."

Joe Sparano, Graphic
Designer and Teacher,
from "Notes on Design"

From manual to automated, slow to fast, the shifts of pace and production in Western culture will continue to transform how older adults like Lam Wei experience daily life, and whether they feel included or excluded by new devices, processes, and spaces. Regardless of the hype around technological advancement, the human desire to have ownership over one's everyday activities, lifestyle choices, and physiological states will remain, presenting a unique opportunity for leveraging technological devices and the IoT.

While some older adults will live and thrive without debilitating conditions affecting their minds and bodies, an overwhelming percentage of the population will develop one or more chronic conditions that will increasingly inhibit their ability to exercise agency over their day-to-day lives. To mitigate the effects of losing mental and/or physical capacities in old age, we must consider what drives older adults' desire for autonomy and how they may want to utilize technology to achieve independence.

EXPERIENCE DRIVERS

Forces Influencing How Older Adults Experience Technology

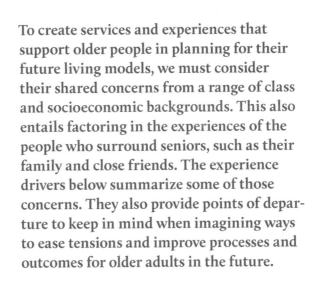

To create services and experiences that support older people in planning for their future living models, we must consider their shared concerns from a range of class and socioeconomic backgrounds. This also entails factoring in the experiences of the people who surround seniors, such as their family and close friends. The experience drivers below summarize some of those concerns. They also provide points of departure to keep in mind when imagining ways to ease tensions and improve processes and outcomes for older adults in the future.

1. Usability and Accessibility

While older adults have a range of capabilities with respect to devices, tools, and other technological interventions, many will require products and services to be highly accessible—in terms of both their physical and cognitive abilities, and their level of experience—and simple to use.

> How can technological tools, particularly those associated with health and well-being, follow a "plug-and-play" model as closely as possible?

2. Consent

Older adults may agree to having their activities and data visible to others, as long as they can do some looking of their own. They will also need to understand the purpose and intent of each new technological intervention they incorporate in their lives.

> How might we design technology that makes explicit the ways in which it is being used, and will continue to be used?

3. Participation

Older adults are often relegated to the sidelines of design, decision making, and implementation in the technology space. It is important for these users to participate in the development of the technological interventions that will affect their daily lives.

> How might devices and applications incorporate principles of universal design, as well as multiple points of access and management?

4. Connection Across Time and Space

Older adults see technology in the same way that many young people do: as a portal to wider worlds, social and otherwise, that are not available in their immediate surroundings.

> How might we consider social needs—and the ethical considerations that they engender—as primary drivers in the use of digital devices or services?

5. Entertainment

Multimedia technology solutions can be important sources of entertainment, particularly for older adults who live alone or have restricted mobility.

> How might we streamline and simplify access to entertainment media to ensure that all users are delighted, inspired, or otherwise entertained, even if they don't have specialized technical knowledge?

OPPORTUNITY SPACE

Rethinking Gerontechnology and Investing in the Right Initiatives

Given the systemic, experiential, and foresight perspectives brought forward, as well as the learnings we captured in our interviews with aging and healthcare experts across North America and Europe, we have defined an opportunity space as a takeaway for this chapter. We use opportunity spaces to capture the key thinking and findings uncovered in our research. These spaces are also intended to inform and inspire organizations across industries to design better futures, in this case, for older adults.

This chapter's opportunity space challenges conventional thinking around how people view and utilize technology to maximize their autonomy and healthspans as they age.

Invest in Technique

Context

In a world that can feel alien and inelegant, individuals desire technologies that have been developed with careful attention to detail. Technology should be fully functional and integrated within people's lives.

Opportunity Space

Explore opportunities to promote a sense of artistry and craftsmanship in technologies developed for older adults. Include this audience as collaborators in the initial design of new technologies, and work to understand what drives these individuals to integrate these technologies into their everyday lives.

Technique is about so much more than being able to carry out a task. It encompasses the complex relationship between the body and mind of a craftsperson—someone who not only does something, but does something with intentionality. In the context of building technologies for older adults, technique is critical. Older people often feel left out, because they are not privy to the thinking behind new consumer or healthcare technologies that have been designed for them. They are excluded from the process of designing these technologies—at least in terms of how they will become a part of their physical, social, and emotional lives.

Because older adults engage with technology in a more values-based way, bring them into the design process early, and give them the skills needed to shape for themselves what the creation, use, and meaning of a new technology will be. This is the best way to overcome the challenge of designing for a unique population, while also recognizing the uniqueness of each individual user.

Reimagining Lam Wei's Story

Throughout this chapter, we explored the current realities and challenges facing older adults in terms of the role technology plays in their lives. We examined why the aging population often feels left when it comes to designing for their technological futures, and we also looked at signals indicating emerging shifts in this perspective.

In closing, we would like to reimagine Lam Wei's story in order to capture some of the ways in which more thoughtful engagement with older adults could contribute to the design of less-intrusive, more integrated technologies. In this version of Lam Wei's story, technology is leveraged during even the most mundane moments of daily living, making it clear how inclusive design could come to shape the ability of aging adults to live independently.

It was Wednesday, but Lam Wei didn't mind hump days like the rest of the world. For her, it was a day to look forward to. Every Wednesday, she would spend half a day working at the family grocery store that she had run all her life. Her daughter, Nikki, was in charge of it now, but Lam Wei helped out three days a week.

She wished she could do more, but her joints weren't what they used to be. And besides, she had other important things to do too, like taking her grandchildren to the park. Still, the store had always felt like home to her. When she had handed it over to Nikki, she'd been relieved that it was staying in the family.

Lam Wei finished her breakfast and took her dishes to the sink. Her automated pill dispenser sensed her presence and played a jingle as it dispersed four multi-colored pills. Lam Wei had set the device up by the sink because she always took her dirty dishes there immediately after eating—she hated leaving a mess—and these pills were to be taken with food. Even though she was usually in a hurry to get somewhere, this setup made it nearly impossible to forget her medication.

As she made the 20-minute walk to the store, Lam Wei checked her phone and saw that Nikki had sent a picture of the kids getting dropped off at school. She would be picking them up later and taking them back to her house. The kids always loved evenings at grandma's; they were allowed to eat egg custard tarts, and they had fun playing in Lam Wei's backyard.

Nikki greeted Lam Wei with a hug and kiss on the cheek when she arrived at the store, 15 minutes before opening.

"Hi, mom. Did you have a nice walk over?"

"I did, sweetie. I think the new meds are working well. My knees are hardly bothering me."

"Great. I'm so glad to hear."

They had set up the pill dispenser to notify Nikki if Lam Wei ever forget to take her pills. Luckily, Nikki hadn't received a single notification yet, which was making her feel much more relaxed about Lam Wei's decision to keep living at home. Nikki had also insisted on having motion detectors installed in the kitchen, an idea that Lam Wei had felt unsure about at first—she didn't want to feel spied on. However, after visiting a showroom and seeing just how uninvasive the detectors were, Lam Wei had finally agreed.

Visiting the showroom was a great experience. Not only had Lam Wei been able to ask questions about how everything worked, but she also got a chance to meet the designers and engineers behind the technology. They customized the monitoring package to her needs by asking about her daily routine, and about what she was struggling with most. They even asked her questions about which features she thought were most important. During this visit, Lam Wei learned that the sensors would be connected to a virtual assistant, which would monitor for alerts and respond by sending help if needed. Now that the sensors had been installed, she had to admit that it gave her some peace of mind knowing that the system was making things easier for Nikki.

Lam Wei's half day at the store went by fast. She ate a light lunch in the break room while Nikki stayed out front, then stopped off at the bakery for the egg tarts and headed to the school. Her two grandchildren ran up to her excitedly, jumping around while talking about their days.

Later that evening, Lam Wei tidied up the kitchen while the children played out back. The pill dispenser played its jingle again and released a different set of pills this time—the ones she needed to take on an empty stomach. She took the pills, then sipped on a glass of water as she stood by the kitchen window of her home, watching her grandchildren play and thinking about how quickly they were growing—and how lucky she was to see it up close.

Economic
Contexts

SYSTEMIC
PERSPECTIVE

Money Matters

Understanding the current state.

"Thou makest me realize the reason why we never found a measure of wealth. We never sought it."

George S. Clason, Author, from *The Richest Man in Babylon*

Tired, overused metaphors such as "Silver Tsunami" and "Gray Workforce" reflect society's attempts to grapple with the economic implications of a growing aging population. As people are living well past retirement age, outdated paradigms of income generation, spending, and wealth management are being put to the test, setting the stage for changes not only to economies at large, but also to the personal income security and independence of older adults at all levels of wealth. The drivers shaping the economic factors tied to aging are multiple, but also interdependent and entangled; as such, they are best thought about together.

Wealth Disparity

The widely held logic is that the aging workforce will affect labor productivity—including how the concept of productivity itself is defined and understood. As the proportion of people past retirement age continues to grow, many are concerned about a subsequent decline in active members of the workforce. This shift in demographics is expected to have profound implications for the role that workforce productivity plays in shaping each individual's personal identity, sense of fulfillment, and perception of their contributions to society. Many also worry that economic growth will stagnate as unemployed seniors draw more from the tax pool than they provide, and as their spending habits change in accordance with their reduced incomes.

For many individuals, their retirement income is, and will continue to be, insufficient—this is particularly true for those who have failed or been unable to prepare through long-term savings and financial planning. This, combined with the fact that public pensions are much less likely to pay out at 100% like they did in the past, is resulting in financial instability for many older adults. Yet, at the same time, there is also a population of wealthy, affluent older adults. Together, this group represents about $8 trillion in economic activity in North America alone—a number larger than the GDP of many countries.

These demographics indicate that, in the near future, there will be a greater number of poorer, less fulfilled seniors. This will likely result in stagnant economic growth, ultimately contributing to a wider gap between the wealthy and the poor. Given that wealth affects health, if not happiness, life expectancy for the affluent will continue to extend, while seniors with lower incomes will be unable to receive the same benefits of advances in longevity science, health, and wellness.

Proactively Preparing for the Economic Future

Despite overwhelming media coverage and research calling attention to the concerns illuminated above, many believe that there is still room for a sense of realistic optimism about the future economy in the context of an aging society. After all, societies have recurrently proven their ability to adapt to major economic and demographic shifts. This adaptation is often the result of a simple change in perspective. In the case of the economic impact of an aging population, this might mean thinking of later life not as a time of decline and need, but as one of abundance and creativity. With this mindset, organizations can focus not on overcoming the "burden" of retired seniors draining the limited well of social resources, but instead on leveraging this growing population in a way that creates positive change for the young and old alike.

Organizations have already reimagined the notion of work to accommodate groups that were not traditionally represented in the typical workplace, including women, parents, members of the LGBTQ community, and millennials. Many organizations are redefining work for older employees as well, resulting in the growing popularity of new terms like "rewirement," "encore career," and "senior-preneur." Further, as the gig and sharing economies expand, and as new types of social services, guaranteed services, retirement products, insurance options, and data-selling opportunities emerge, people will continue to benefit from entirely new income streams.

In this chapter, we will explore how long-held notions of workforce participation, spending, retirement, and investment are changing, and how they will continue to change at an unprecedented rate to accommodate the aging population. We will also examine the different pathways that organizations in the longevity economy can pursue to promote growth, rather than accepting stagnation.

In the case of the economic impact of an aging population, [a change in perspective] might mean thinking of later life not as a time of decline and need, but as one of abundance and creativity.

EXPERIENTIAL INSIGHT

The Experience of Economic Contribution

Exploring the context of financial status and planning

"It is the character of lived experience I want to explore, not the nature of man."

Michael D. Jackson, Poet and Anthropologist, from *Paths Towards a Clearing*

Older adults planning for their financial futures are well aware of the contradictions in today's socioeconomic climate. Advances in health sciences may allow them to live longer, but this longevity is likely to come with more debilitating (and often expensive) medical conditions. Many people who have spent their lives investing time and money in social, financial, and government institutions have seen these institutions stagnate, falter, or even dissolve. Older people are remaining in the workforce past traditional retirement age, while offices and factory floors alike are increasingly turning to outsourcing, contract workers, or automation.

Like the economy itself, the ways in which older adults think about money and plan for their futures are anything but predictable. For some, old age is about balancing fixed incomes and the high cost of healthcare. Others are wealthier than they ever expected to be in their youth, raising concerns about how to divide their wealth over time and among family members. Regardless of their circumstances, the next generation of older adults must manage their personal finances and make decisions that impact their own lives and the lives of their loved ones.

Inequality

The term "inequality" is often used to refer to disparities between rich and poor. However, the matter of who "has" or "has not," and the relationship between these two groups, is only one component of inequality. There are important distinctions between income inequality and wealth inequality, which have different causes and impacts. There are also many overlaps between economic inequality and other forms of social, racial, geographic, ability, and class-based inequities that powerfully affect how people experience the world.

Nuances associated with inequality are especially relevant to older people, who are more likely to sit at the extreme ends of economic stratification and to be impacted by money concerns on a daily basis. Because

Nuances associated with inequality are especially relevant to older people, who are more likely to sit at the extreme ends of economic stratification and to be impacted by money concerns on a daily basis.

they have had more time than most to accumulate wealth or debt, and will generally have less time to be active in the workplace, most older people are fixed into a class or economic category and do not see themselves as mobile across those categories. Disadvantaged seniors—that is, those who also suffer additional forms of discrimination—are clearly impacted the most by disparities in wealth. However, middle-class and wealthy older adults may also experience stresses associated with living in an unequal society.

While there are as many ways to manage finances as there are people, older adults across the economic spectrum are developing new ways of thinking about, dealing with, and distributing their money. Though such new behaviors do not necessarily challenge current social and economic hierarchies, they do work to address and ameliorate individual stresses, which can help dull the sharpest edges of inequality.

"Furthermore, if people of high socioeconomic status are living longer and healthier lives while people of low socioeconomic status are living longer but in poor health, the negative consequences of a generic policy response, such as increasing the pension age, will be shared inequitably."

WHO, *World Report on Ageing and Health* (2015)

Work and Income Security

The old-age dependency ratio was once a trusted tool used to project the relationship between working adults (ages 15–64) and non-working adults (65 and over). Today, researchers and analysts across fields find this tool to be outdated and limited, as it is no longer reasonable or accurate to assume that all people will retire at age 65. In response, the World Bank has adopted an "adult dependency ratio" that addresses the distinctions between "active" and "non-active" working adults, with the aim of including older workers and accurately documenting the workplace.

Many people are continuing to work because they are living longer than they imagined and have less savings than they thought they would need. Whether it is due to a lifetime of low-wage work that has made it impossible to save, a financial crash that has disrupted plans, a divorce that has split assets, or adult children who need help with their own finances, many older adults are finding that they want or need to continue earning money. For some, however, working longer is a choice rather than a necessity. These individuals continue working because they value a set schedule, or because they crave the purpose and social activity that their working life affords them. The increased popularity of working from home or pursuing jobs in the gig economy also offers new possibilities for older adults who don't want to give up their working lives but who need jobs that also meet their other needs.

While the impacts of ageism and related discrimination in many kinds of workplaces should not be underestimated, expectations around retirement have nevertheless changed drastically for the poor, the wealthy, and everyone in between—and the decision-making processes of older adults surrounding how they want to live have followed suit.

Spending Patterns

The spending of US residents ages 50 and up accounts for more than $8 trillion in economic activity. The Boston Consulting Group predicts that by 2030, US residents aged 55 and over will account for 50% of all domestic consumer spending growth. In Japan, this proportion is expected to rise to 67%, while Germany should anticipate this rate reaching 86% in the same time frame. To successfully adapt to this increased spending power, organizations across industries will need to rethink their preconceived notions about the needs and desires of these consumers.

Older adults are buying into various consumer trends, products, and services that go far beyond meeting basic physiological or safety needs. They have higher-level, more dynamic drives that shape their spending behavior, including lifelong goals and dreams, unfulfilled aspirations, as well as aesthetic passions and preferences. They also continue to invest in the different communities to which they belong by spending on their spouses, children, siblings, friends, and other members of their social networks. Viewing older adults as profoundly engaged, passionate, and opinionated consumers means setting aside the rhetoric of burden, decline, and dependence so often used to describe this group. To meaningfully reshape the economics of aging in the future, we must recognize older adults as possessing agency and power over the economic reality of the next century.

Viewing older adults as profoundly engaged, passionate, and opinionated consumers means setting aside the rhetoric of burden, decline, and dependence so often used to describe this group.

Investments +
Planning

The global financial crisis of 2008 made it impossible for people to take economic stability for granted, even in countries with robust patterns of growth and long histories of stable inflation. While it's always a gamble to invest in or plan for a particular financial future, this particular crisis laid bare the fragility of previously unquestioned tools used to mitigate risk. People became uncertain of their pensions, mortgages, and even their banks, leading many to begin depending on more social forms of investment. With this shift, many people began planning their futures around relationships, social institutions, and collective forms of wealth that they anticipated as being more predictable and stable over time.

Older adults are experienced social investors. Only some have played the stock market or financed startups, but all have spent their lives contributing—through taxes, volunteering, or other engagements—to local infrastructure, workplace benefits, social welfare systems, and/or global initiatives. Many have also invested heavily in their children and grandchildren, whether motivated by the promise of emotional or monetary returns.

Older people know more than most that it is impossible to predict the future. Nevertheless, this group will continue to seek products and services that help them envision and create the future they desire.

"**Private pensions in OECD countries reported $4 trillion USD in losses in asset values in the first 10 months of 2008. [...] Including other private pension assets in voluntary personal plans in the United States (such as IRAs) and in other countries, the loss increases to about $5 trillion USD.**"

Gregorio Impavido and Ian Tower, "How the Financial Crisis Affects Pensions and Insurance and Why the Impacts Matter," *The International Monetary Fund*

Alex's Story

Bringing to life current challenges in financial status and planning.

To help bring to life the concepts explored through-out this book, we have created personas for each chapter. A persona grounds ethnographic research within an individual narrative and reveals how overarching themes may play out for a particular person.

The persona for this chapter is a character named Alex, whose story is intended to bring to life insights about how older adults navigate different economic challenges. Here, we look at how the challenges discussed so far may manifest in Alex's life. At the end of the chapter, we will see another version of Alex's story: one in which some of the possibilities discussed throughout this chapter have been enacted, resulting in an improved experience of aging for Alex.

Alex is a retired teacher in his late sixties. He lives in Michigan with his wife, Helen, a retired postal worker. They have three grown children who live independently. Four years ago, Helen fell and broke her hip while cleaning the driveway. She soon retired, taking the accident as a sign that it was time to slow down, and Alex joined her after finishing the school year. The couple's pensions have allowed them to continue paying their mortgage, which they've nearly paid off entirely over 25 years. In the past couple years, Alex has been struggling through the harsh Michigan winters due to his worsening asthma. He and Helen have been considering spending their winters in Florida. Their daughter, Kayla, is also getting married soon, and the couple would like to help pay for her wedding. Alex and Helen are reluctant to refinance their home, but it seems like the best way to accommodate their financial needs.

The story below represents a brief glimpse into Alex's life, including the challenges he faces when making decisions about his financial situation.

Alex sat at the kitchen table with a notepad, pencil, and calculator in front of him. He coughed lightly into the crook of his elbow as he stared down at the numbers he had written out. *There must be a way to make this work*, he thought to himself.

His wife came into the kitchen with her cell phone pressed to her ear. It didn't take Alex very long to figure out that she was talking to their daughter, Kayla.

"Mmhm," Helen said as she pulled out a chair to join him at the table. "Uh-huh. No, I agree, you have to send real thank-you cards. I'm just not sure they need to be custom made."

Alex rolled his eyes at Helen, gesturing dramatically down at the budget he had drawn up. His wife put up her hands defensively and mouthed something at him: *I know, I know.*

After saying goodbye to Kayla, Helen ran her fingers through her hair and let out an exasperated sigh. "Maybe I should have gone back to work after the accident," she said, sounding defeated. She looked up at Alex. "Do you think they would take me back at this point? I'm only 68—I'm still young. I can deliver mail with the best of them."

Alex reached out and clasped his wife's hand. "Honey, I say this with love: 68 is not young."

Helen scoffed. "The nerve!" she cried, pretending to be offended.

Alex's booming laugh was quickly cut short by a harsh, dry cough, which sent him into an intense wheezing spell. Before he knew it, Helen was at his side holding an inhaler to his mouth and calmly rubbing his back. As the fit subsided, Alex found himself facing the same realization he'd had over a month ago, when the first cold front had nearly sent him to the hospital: *I can't handle this much longer.*

"We can tell Kayla that we have a budget for her wedding," Helen said. "If she wants to have this big to-do, she's going to have to pay for most of it herself."

"Absolutely not," Alex responded. "It's important to her, Helen. And I know it's important to you, too."

"But sweetheart, we have to get you somewhere warmer next winter. This just isn't sustainable. And I could certainly do with some sunshine, too. As my husband likes to remind me, I'm an old lady now. Plus, who knows when that devious driveway of ours will make its next move? It snuck up on me once before, you know."

Alex stared down at the paper in front of him. He knew what he and Helen had to do, but he couldn't bring himself to say it out loud. They had worked so hard for so long. When he was a teacher, he had spent his summers doing landscaping, and Helen had worked as much as she could while being the primary caregiver for their three kids. As a teacher, Alex had always impressed upon his children the importance of having an education. So, when the kids all pursued undergraduate degrees—and even later, when their son Blake had decided on graduate school—Alex and Helen had contributed as much as they could. They'd even loaned their oldest son money for his first house, all while paying down their own mortgage.

Even now, Alex could hear his late father's voice in his head. *You have to own your home*, he had said. *You work hard, you put a good roof over your family's head, and by the time you're an old man like me, you'll have a house that no one can take away from you. A house you can be proud of.*

Alex felt like he and Helen had done everything right, but the numbers in front of him were telling a different story: It still wasn't enough.

"Helen," Alex said, his voice serious, "We can do it all. But we have to get a reverse mortgage."

Transforming How We Navigate Economic Contribution

The future of financial status and planning in later life.

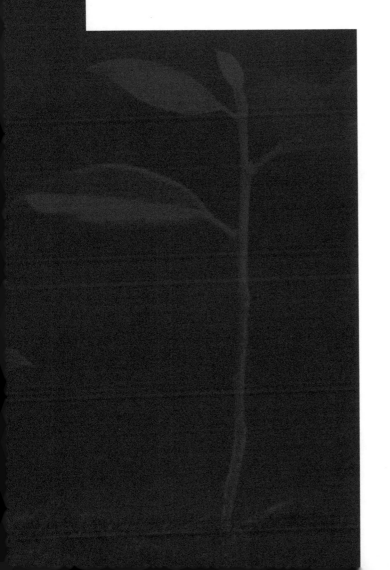

"Traditional assumptions—that learning ends in one's 20s, career progression ends in the 40s, and work ends in the 60s—are no longer accurate or sustainable."

Dimple Argawal et al.,
"The Longevity Dividend,"
Deloitte Insights

To understand how the aging population will contend with changing resources and opportunities, we must first identify and articulate "shifts"—that is, large-scale transitions taking place within society today. Throughout this book, we use these shifts to help articulate the tensions that emerged during our foresight research. We performed diverse scanning of various moments of change influencing Western society, whether those came in the form of a film, article, tech startup, or conversation. Shifts allow us to frame new questions and establish future-oriented points of view, which can in turn help us imagine and create more meaningful realities for aging individuals.

SHIFT 1

From Retiring

to Working Longer to Retain Purpose in Life

More older adults are staying in the workforce longer—whether because they need to, because their work provides a sense of purpose, or both. Knowing as we do now that a sense of purpose improves well-being, society is redefining both retirement and what it means to work in later life.

"It's not that you have to work forever... but those who retire too early [can] feel more sad and lonely and disconnected."

Esteban Calvo, Sociologist and Epidemiologist, in Tara Bahrampour's "This Is Your Brain on Retirement—Not Nearly as Sharp, Studies Are Finding," *The Washington Post*

> Purpose Over Pleasure

A century ago, living to age 65 was the rare exception rather than the rule. Today, however, life expectancy for North Americans has reached the high seventies and early eighties, with many living well into their nineties. This begs the question: What will people do with these extra years of life? While there are certainly older North Americans who have worked, saved, and invested, and are now looking forward to the prospect of self-improvement and personal growth in retirement, there are also many people of retirement age who need to continue working well past their sixties out of financial necessity. Then, there are the lucky few who have chosen to continue working because they enjoy it, or because their work is core to their identity. For this minority, research reveals some good news: Working longer can be good for one's health. This is because work—especially work that one enjoys—is mentally and socially engaging, which increases an individual's sense of identity and self-worth.

> "...32% of the income of elderly Americans derives from work, compared to 20% of that of Italians and only 13% of the Germans. It seems that Americans work more—and depend to a greater extent on working for their identity as well as for their income—than Europeans."
>
> Dr. Muriel Gillick, MD and Author, from *Life in the End Zone*

Intentional Endeavors more than Aspirations of Relaxation

Over the past few decades, investment advisors have sold a retirement dream rooted in the idea of financial security. After retiring comfortably between the ages of 55 and 65, the story goes, older adults will be free to enjoy a life of leisure on the golf course or to travel the world. The assigning of 65 as the universal retirement age goes all the way back to 1905, when the idea was popularized by Dr. William Osler. He believed that workers aged 25 to 40 were in peak form; that those between 40 and 60 were tolerable, but uncreative; and that anyone over 60 was not useful to society. Over a century later, today's older adults are finding deep purpose in their work later in life—and contributing value that proves they are anything but useless.

Having the freedom to enjoy life by participating in recreational activities is often not as satisfying as one might expect. On the contrary, not having a reason to get out of bed in the morning can cause existential pain, while working longer can provide a much needed sense of purpose in later life. In their study, "Purpose in Life as a Psychosocial Resource in Healthy Aging," Fogelman and Canli found that a person's cortisol level,

Not having a reason to get out of bed in the morning can cause existential pain, while working longer can provide a much needed sense of purpose in later life.

which is an indicator of stress, increases as purpose in life decreases. Those seniors choosing to work past the typical retirement age could enjoy a healthier, longer life as a result.

Today, work practices are beginning to change to accommodate many relatively "new" demographic groups that did not previously enjoy full participation in the labor force, including millennials, parents, and—most recently—older employees. They are demanding more flexibility, a shorter work week, and a retirement track that emphasizes slowing down, transitioning, or making a significant career change rather than encouraging a hard stop at an arbitrary age like 65. With people working past retirement age, and with technology expected to replace many existing jobs, new types of jobs are emerging—jobs designed to meet the needs and utilize the skills of older workers, offered by companies that don't simply dismiss seniors as useless, out of touch, or overqualified.

SIGNALS

#1

Encore Facilitators

Rather than sailing into the sunset and enjoying retirement, many seniors are pursuing encore careers. Encore.org, a nonprofit organization, helps connect retirees with projects that create lasting social value. By challenging the socially accepted activities usually associated with retirement, Encore.org promotes the idea of a "second act": an opportunity to provide a service to society after retirement through passionate engagement in projects that benefit one's community. The socially driven organization claims to be building a movement that taps into the skills and experience of those in midlife and beyond to improve communities and the world.

#2

Welcoming Older Workers

Though many employers perceive older workers as a burden, there are some notable exceptions. In Germany, BMW invested significant capital to modify a division of one of its assembly lines in order to better accommodate older workers. Changes made included installing larger computer screens with bigger type, providing employees with special shoes for aching feet, and adding chairs to some parts of the line so workers can perform tasks while sitting down. In the US, outdoor apparel retailer L.L. Bean recruits retirees for seasonal jobs in the company's call centers, distribution facility, and flagship store. The organization finds that retirees bring a high level of maturity and a strong work ethic, and they are able to commit to inconsistent work schedules.

SHIFT 2

From Purchasing Power through Pensions and Savings

to Economic Insecurity

People are living longer, but without pensions and savings, can they afford to? In the near future, there will be more adults in retirement than youth in the workforce. We'll need creative solutions to ensure these shifting demographics do not become a threat to economic stability.

"The financial crisis has bolstered people's support for pensions... 82% of people in the US think a pension is worth having and 67% say they would take less pay to get a guaranteed income at retirement."

Janet Guyon, Editor, "Jobs at These 10 Companies Will Literally Pay You for Life," *Quartz*

66

"If aging boomers have it so good, why do Social Security benefits comprise more than half of family budgets for 44% of lead-ing-edge boomers, ages 65 to 69, who've filed for benefits?"

Chris Farrell, Columnist and Author, "No, Boomers Aren't What's Wrong with the Economy," *Forbes*

Hidden Realities

The "silver economy" is a term that refers to how baby boomers represent one of the biggest, most powerful, and most prosperous segments driving the economy. Considering this phenomenon, many believe that any company not actively designing, building, and marketing for this population is miss-ing out on a huge opportunity. Even with more savings and fewer expenses than their younger peers, baby boomers (born between 1946 and 1964) are notoriously slippery consumers. They are looking to spend more on experiences, such as travel and entertain-ment, but also on caregiving, and they aim to spend less on physical products.

Indeed, many of today's aging adults have benefited from inflated real estate, generous pensions, and investment portfolios over the course of their working lives. However, as class divisions continue to grow, so too does the likelihood of a poor economic outlook for older adults—even for some of today's boom-ers. Huge disparities already exist within this cohort of people. Contrary to popular belief, many in this age group are econom-ically insecure. According to the Insured Retirement Institute, this is in part because 70% of baby boomers in the US falsely believe that they can survive off Social Security. As a result, they have not benefited as much as they could have from savings, pensions, or from the period of relative economic stability during which they were employed.

> Dancing with Debt Instead of Relaxing on Financial Safety Nets

Security in old age is often associated with savings and a stable pension, the result of years of work in the same position with the same company. Twenty years ago, most older adults entered retirement debt free; today, more and more are taking on debt, whether for mortgages, renovations, or to pay down bills. In the US, those over 60 have over $67 trillion worth of debt. This explosion in debt is driving fears that economic insecurity will only get worse as populations age and the workforce shrinks.

As work is changing, more people of all ages are working inconsistently in casual, part-time, and low-wage jobs, leaving many with no savings or guaranteed incomes from company pensions. According to a report by JPMorgan Chase Institute, roughly 1% of older adults in the US—that is, over 400,000 individuals—are participating in the gig economy. Even those with regular employment aren't saving as much as they used to; despite being encouraged to save and make regular contributions to pension plans, 31% of working-age Americans don't have a pension or savings, according to the Federal Reserve, and almost 50% of Americans could not come up with $400 to pay for an emergency, writes Neil Gabler in his article for *The Atlantic*, "The Secret Shame of Middle Class Americans." If so many people can't find a little extra money for a month, how

When social systems fail to address economic insecurity among the elderly, the consequences are dire, and the solutions inconsistent.

will they ever finance a longer lifespan than anticipated?

Though some researchers and policy analysts have suggested raising the eligibility age for retirement or Social Security and cutting government spending on health and social services, this would do little more than shift the burden of support to individuals and families. Changes such as these would threaten people's health, as financial security is still the most important indicator of long-term health. There is a huge life-expectancy discrepancy between the rich and poor. In her article for *The New York Times*, "Income Inequality Grows With Age and Shapes Later Life," columnist Paula Span cites a startling statistic: Whereas the wealthy have gained an extra 13 years of life, on average, since 1960, the poor have only gained 4 years. When social systems fail to address economic insecurity among the elderly, the consequences are dire, and the solutions inconsistent. In Japan, for example, those struggling to support themselves on

meager pensions sometimes steal food in an attempt to be arrested and placed in one of the country's "comfortable" prisons. In England, on the other hand, one food bank café provides malnourished seniors with food otherwise destined for the landfill.

There are, however, a few notable instances of governments and businesses prioritizing longer-term planning over stop-gap measures. More specifically, some institutions are attempting to address the demographic imbalance by increasing the number of workers contributing to the tax base in order to support older adults in need of pensions. In Denmark, for instance, the government is attempting to raise the birth rate by encouraging mothers to send their adult children on baby-making vacations. Other proposed solutions include a universal basic income (UBI), which a number of countries are experimenting with, either in addition to or as a replacement for pension plans.

SIGNALS

#1

Thinking Collectively

UBI, where a government provides a small income to all citizens with no strings attached, is not a new idea. However, it has gained significant attention as a potential income-security strategy in recent years—particularly in response to fears that automation will result in mass job loss. Governments and humanitarian organizations believe they have a duty to support those who are struggling. In a 2007 review of their own aid strategies, UNICEF recognized that "cash transfers are consistent with the human rights-based approach [because] cash (unlike food aid) empowers people to determine their own priorities and meet their own basic needs." Though Ontario recently cancelled a pilot study to assess how UBI affects its recipients' health, work effort, and housing status, other countries (including Finland, Germany, California, and Kenya) are going ahead with their pilots. Researchers are hopeful that the results will show that giving cash without strings attached is an effective welfare and anti-poverty strategy.

#2

Living for Today, Planning for Tomorrow

The desire to live for now can conflict with the need to proactively plan for the future—a future in which many will struggle to remain financially independent. In Canada, Bonnie-Jeanne MacDonald, from the National Institute on Ageing at Ryerson University, has proposed a financial instrument called Living Income For the Elderly (LIFE). LIFE would be a completely voluntary, government-led, pooled-risk fund. The plan would require amended legislation that allows people to invest in a deferred annuity at 65, with payouts beginning at age 85. With more than half of today's 65-year-old North Americans expected to live to 85, this plan would allow retirees to turn their savings into an income stream at a low cost. The benefit would be real financial independence, as the financial risks associated with LIFE would not be picked up or navigated by younger Canadians.

SHIFT 3

From Intergenerational Divisions

to Cross-Generational Class Consciousness

Today, younger generations are reluctant to pay benefits for adults in retirement—especially for members of this older cohort who have benefited from a period of economic prosperity. However, as the income gap continues to widen across all generations, class is coming to define people's experiences more than age.

"Boomers have no doubt benefited from their incredible electoral clout, but as the old truism goes, the rich are getting richer, and the poor are getting more screwed, no matter what age they are."

Bridie Jabour, Author, "Boomers and Millennials: This Is not Intergenerational Warfare, It's Class Warfare," *The Guardian*

> Supporting Your Neighbor Instead of Resenting Differences

> Class Conflict

Much has been made of intergenerational conflict. From the blaming of boomers to the maligning of millennials, generational differences have been linked to a clash of values, practices, and attitudes. Workplaces and family homes alike have been the battle-grounds for disagreements over communi-cation styles (and methods), spending habits, work ethics, and planning (or not planning) for the future. Recently, however, intergen-erational conflict has become as much about economic challenges as it is about culture clash, at least in some parts of the world. Young people can't help but feel as though the jobs, resources, and financial security they were promised and have worked hard for have all but disappeared, having been (irresponsibly) used up by the generations that came before them.

Young people of working age can hardly be blamed for the common perception that they have lost out on resources that were once abundant. While some of the wealth disparity between cohorts can be attributed to seniors' financially disciplined outlook and behavior, the larger concentra-tion of wealth among older people is also largely a feature of public policy and good timing. Since the 1970s, there has been a major change in the prospective fortunes of younger and older people in North America. In Canada, seniors were enacting their Depression-era values and socking away money for a rainy day just as they were receiving a major boost from the intro-duction of public benefits like the Canada Pension Plan, Old Age Security, and taxpay-er-funded healthcare. Additionally, many Canadian seniors were spared the brunt of the 2008 meltdown because they had already shifted their savings into low-risk investments when they retired, says Goshka Folda, Senior Managing Director of research firm Investor Economics. All this adds up to some legitimate disparity along generational lines. In the 1980s, the typical senior was four times wealthier than the average twenty-something. Today's seniors are, on average, nine times richer than their millennial grandchildren.

And yet, even as a large group of North American seniors have been able to amass wealth, elderly people in general are still far more vulnerable to poverty and economic disenfranchisement than their younger counterparts. In Canada, for instance, the median after-tax income for unattached seniors was $26,100 in 2016, only slightly above the defined low-income measure of $22,133. In the US, half of all people 65 and older had less than $23,394 in income. In other parts of the world, such as Hong Kong, Australia, and South Korea, poverty among the elderly has become the norm. As people have become more aware of the root causes and impacts of poverty, cross-generational movements against gentrification and the rising cost of public transit have emerged, and support for healthcare reform has grown. In the lead-up to the 2016 US Presidential Election, support for Bernie Sanders—who promised to eliminate student debt and strengthen social security—came from both old and young Americans, indicating that future issues will run directly through generational lines instead of across them.

As people have become more aware of the root causes and impacts of poverty, cross-generational movements against gentrification and the rising cost of public transit have emerged, and support for healthcare reform has grown.

SIGNALS

#1

Intergenerational Mashups and Alliances

In some parts of the world, cross-generational collaboration is entering spaces where physical and financial well-being overlap in powerful ways. Inspired by the lack of affordable housing for both students and seniors in Toronto, the HomeShare Pilot Program is pairing students with seniors in mutually beneficial living arrangements. In exchange for subsidized rent, university students provide company and practical support to their senior roommates. As mentioned in Chapter One, in the Netherlands, students receive free accommodation in nursing homes in exchange for providing care to senior residents. Another example is Providence Mount St. Vincent in Seattle, which is a nursing home where residents and staff share their 300,000 square-foot facility with a daycare five days a week. This childcare is part of the Mount's Intergenerational Learning Center (ILC), where nursing home residents are welcome to observe in the classrooms, and structured activities between children and residents are scheduled daily.

#2

Age-Agnostic Entrepreneurship

Intergenerational entrepreneurship is becoming increasingly common. This practice may lead to business success for innovators, and it also has the potential to solve a number of challenges for several generations. OneClick.chat, for instance, is an app that provides video chat services for businesses. Co-founders Dillon Meyers and Alan Gibson—a millennial and a baby boomer, respectively—designed the app with accessibility across generations in mind. For instance, they recently partnered with Georgia Tech to provide affordable and accessible interactive video services for older adults with disabilities. The company was even awarded a grant from the National Institutes of Health, two-thirds of which was provided by the National Institute of Aging.

SHIFT 4

Investing in the Future: From Financial

to Social Legacies

Individuals who live longer lives may require more care in their later years, which means more expenses. For these individuals, the act of leaving a financial legacy may seem less realistic and less meaningful than leaving a social legacy: one that impacts their family, community, and/or a political and social group.

66

"The beauty of thinking about your legacy is that it forces you to frame your decisions and actions beyond just yourself in order to include how you affect others, both now and in the future."

James M. Kouzes & Barry Z. Posner, Authors, from *A Leader's Legacy*

> The New Status Marker: Changemaking (not Wealth)

Bestowing Opportunity

In the late 1940s, psychologists Erik and Joan Erikson popularized the idea that one's sense of identity progresses through the life cycle. They believed that later life is a time of generativity, and that during this time, the impulse to give back becomes an urgent need. Recent research supports this notion; studies indicate that the closer people get to death, the more likely they are to consider their legacy, and the more motivated they become to do things that will benefit others in the future. Leaving a legacy is usually a generous act inspired by a sense of responsibility and affinity with someone who won't necessarily reciprocate this generosity. Trust funds, life insurance policies, investments, and the distribution of material possessions are all steps older people can take to ensure that their wealth benefits others in the future. Today, rather than leaving money or other financial tokens, some seniors are embracing the chance to "leave opportunity" by providing their children (as well as the children of others) with a social legacy.

Older adults—both those who were never activists, and those who have been activists for decades—are noting how old age has enhanced their feelings of being disenfranchised and given them more to get angry about. For many, the choice to make their mark as activists rather than financiers is simple. They are especially vulnerable to financial and political shifts, particularly when facing limited or costly access to healthcare, and are also more likely than other cohorts to slip into poverty when economic conditions worsen. From Greek pensioners protesting austerity measures in Athens, to World War II veterans joining the demonstrations of Occupy Wall Street, older people who are economically marginalized are turning their misfortune into an opportunity to make societal change.

"Rosa Parks moments," where seemingly ordinary people choose to act courageously for social change and out of a sense of civic responsibility, are not limited to the economically marginalized. There are certainly some altruistic individuals with financial means who are taking a philanthropic view to retirement planning and thinking beyond their individual assets. Americans gave $300 billion to charity in 2015, and while the poorest

Americans gave 3.2% of their income to charity and the rich only gave 1.3% (according to a 2013 article in *The Atlantic*, "Why the Rich Don't Give to Charity"), some wealthy individuals want to give knowing their donations will have a lasting social impact.

Inspired by this sentiment and looking to encourage philanthropy among the world's super wealthy, Bill Gates, Melinda Gates, and Warren Buffett conceived of a Giving Pledge for Billionaires in 2010. The pledge now has 187 signees, all of whom have committed to giving at least one half of their wealth to causes such as poverty alleviation, refugee aid, disaster relief, global health, education, women and girls' empowerment, medical research, arts and culture, criminal justice reform, and environmental sustainability. They have also committed to improving the professionalism and scale of the Bill & Melinda Gates Foundation. Other aging business leaders are also striving to create more sustainable business models with the goal of establishing a lasting legacy. For example, Patagonia founder Yvon Chouinard has achieved brand recognition for the quality

"Rosa Parks moments," where seemingly ordinary people choose to act courageously for social change and out of a sense of civic responsibility, are not limited to the economically marginalized.

and sustainability of his company's products, and Gunter Pauli, author of *The Blue Economy*, conceived of a new business model to inspire environmentally conscious innovation that looks to a sustainable future. As businesses increasingly strive to implement sustainable business models, to achieve B Corporation status (a certification indicating high standards of social diversity, environmental engagement, transparency, and accountability), or to commit to the principles of the circular economy, many are motivated by a desire to leave a legacy that ensures a healthy and productive future for many generations to come.

"Generativity means giving back without needing anything in return... the form of giving back can be creative, social, personal, or financial."

Daniel Goleman, Author and
Science Journalist, Excerpt from
"The Science of Older and Wiser,"
The New York Times

SIGNALS

#1

Ethical Wills

Even in traditional investing circles, the elderly are being increasingly encouraged to consider what they want to leave behind, both tangible and intangible. This practice has given rise to what some call an "ethical will." This is not a legal document, but rather a letter, video, or audio recording that communicates a person's values, family history, and wisdom so that this can be passed down from one generation to the next. With an ethical will, a person can tell the story of their life, give a rationale for the decisions outlined in their legal will, explain the origins of their precious possessions, share their wishes for the future, or even request forgiveness or articulate burial wishes, among other things. By recording what matters most to them, aging adults can make sense of their lives, ultimately making it easier to accept death with the understanding that they will be remembered as having made a difference during their lives.

#2

Building Better Futures

While the traditional stock market is driven primarily by shareholders' desire for wealth maximization, today, many older adults—a disproportionate number of them women—are looking to invest in businesses that prioritize the long-term health of people and the planet rather than short-term financial returns. While socially oriented businesses are still few and far between, more are being created all the time. B Lab, a global non-profit organization, has been offering B Corps certification since 2009 to help investors distinguish between organizations that merely see an opportunity to make money through green washing and those committed to rethinking business as a force for good. To be certified, social enterprises must demonstrate that they also create value for non-shareholding stakeholders, and that they are committed to social and environmental performance, public transparency, and legal accountability. Today, more than 230 businesses have been certified. While most are relatively small, Patagonia, Ben & Jerry's, and Danone North America are among the notable exceptions.

Bringing to Life the Future of Economic Contribution

Building out possible concepts and solutions.

"In many ways, aging is a personal concern, but coping with this demographic shift will not come down to individual effort. Rather, it's going to take a comprehensive approach—on the part of cities, communities, and companies—to make room for a population that has much to offer, and that we all, someday, will be a part of."

Eillie Anzioltti, from
"Our Aging Population
Can People an Economic
Powerhouse—If We Let
It," *Fast Company*

Economic shifts, as well as the social and political changes that precipitate and follow them, will create a range of potential risks for older adults to navigate in the future. Individuals may need to cope with changes in employment status, with financial anxieties, and with the complex task of managing their money while experiencing illness and physical decline. Despite these changes, some desires and goals will remain fixed, including the basic need to feel secure and the desire to make a meaningful contribution to society both during one's life and after one has passed. In the near future, many older adults will have benefited from high-paying careers and access to services that have helped them manage their finances; however, many others will struggle through economic insecurity and feel a lack of purpose. By understanding the drivers of financial status and planning for aging adults, we can begin to design more secure and purposeful experiences in later life.

EXPERIENCE DRIVERS

Forces Influencing How Older Adults Experience Financial Status and Planning

To create services and experiences that support older people in planning for their futures, we must consider which concerns are shared across socioeconomic backgrounds. This also entails factoring in the experiences of the people who surround older adults, such as their family and close friends. The experience drivers below summarize some of those concerns. They also provide points of departure to keep in mind when imagining ways to ease tensions and improve processes and outcomes for older adults in the future.

1. Security

For older people, financial security is not about predicting the future, but about diminishing risks and preventing the need to develop a financial plan under a new set of pressures.

> How might financial products and services for older people be flexible and/or modular enough to be applied in a variety of circumstances?

2. Recognition

All people value being recognized for what they have built, supported, or contributed to. Older people simply have more that they can be recognized for, and they would benefit from the enhanced social status or more practical outcomes that could come with recognition.

> How might public and private institutions more frequently and more formally recognize older people for the paid and unpaid work that they have done?

3. Legacy

Legacy planning is not just about money, and it not just for the wealthy. It is about honoring the need people have to be remembered in particular ways after they are gone.

> How can our understanding of legacy planning be expanded in a way that helps us consider the environmental, social, and emotional legacies that people may want to leave behind?

OPPORTUNITY SPACE

Rethinking Financial Status and Investing in the Right Initiatives

Given the systemic, experiential, and foresight perspectives brought forward in this chapter, as well as the learnings we captured in our interviews with aging and healthcare experts across North America and Europe, we have defined an opportunity space as a takeaway. We use opportunity spaces to capture the key thinking and findings uncovered in our research. These spaces are also intended to inform and inspire organizations across industries to design better futures, in this case, for older adults.

This chapter's opportunity space surrounding economic contexts intends to challenge conventional thinking around how people think about and navigate financial status and legacy planning as they age.

Invest in Respect

Context

In a world that can feel uncertain and rife with various forms of inequality, individuals desire economic systems that make space for and provide service to everyone, regardless of age or socioeconomic status.

Opportunity Space

Explore opportunities to provide feelings of care and consideration in economic contexts concerning older adults.

Because wealth and income disparity are often the result of social, cultural, and political inequity, it is essential that we provide agency to those working to overcome these forces. This means being realistic about that future—especially when it comes to the kinds of promises made around financial products and services geared toward older adults.

To be realistic means to personalize, to avoid bold proclamations, and to help people assess what's possible for their long-term savings and financial planning. Yet, being realistic does not have to come at the cost of finding revolutionary solutions for addressing the wants, needs, and desires that seniors have regarding their financial lives. With this approach, we can shape a much different and more meaningful framework for helping aging adults prosper—with or without all the money in the world.

Reimagining Alex's Story

Throughout this chapter, we explored the current realities and challenges facing older adults in the context of economics, including work, financial management, and what it means to remain productive during one's later years.

In closing, we would like to reimagine Alex's story to explore ways in which he might become more independent, continue to help others, and engage in intergenerational modes of teaching and collaboration. In this version of Alex's story, he has benefitted from more dynamic, fluid modes of personal and financial growth, allowing him to feel productive while also maintaining the level of financial stability he values.

"Helen? I'm home," Alex called as he closed the front door behind him. Just as Alex bent to take off his shoes, Helen appeared from around the corner. Her brown hair was pulled back in a bun, with loose pieces flying out in all directions, and the apron she wore was covered in flour.

"Hi honey," she said. "How as your walk?"

"It was good," Alex said, smiling. "I had a nice chat with Luis while he was waiting for the bus. When I reminded him that we have a tutoring session after school, he suddenly took great interest in his sneakers."

Helen laughed. "Are you still on your mission to get that boy interested in school, or have you given up on that particular quest?"

"Of course I haven't given up!" Alex said, feigning shock. "I've never given up on a student in my life. Don't you worry—by the time June rolls around, Luis will be begging for summer school. Which he of course won't need this year."

"Good to know you're still so humble, professor."

"Luis is a good kid," Alex said, his tone more serious now. "He just needs a bit of extra help. Reminds me of Blake sometimes, actually."

Helen stepped closer to her husband and gave him a kiss on the cheek. "Oh, don't remind me. That boy sure did give us a run for our money. I hope you're hungry, by the way. I'm making raspberry crepes."

Alex wiped a smudge of flour from his wife's face. "Yes, I can see that. Are we celebrating something with this fancy breakfast, or did the berries just call to you at the market yesterday?"

"Both," Helen said, grinning up at her husband. "Matt just called—he and Georgia are driving down with the kids for a visit in February. They want to stay for a whole week! Oh, and Kayla texted to let me know that she and

Jayden managed to get the guest list down to 160."

Alex kissed Helen on the forehead. "Well then, crepes it is."

After breakfast, Alex sat at the kitchen table with his laptop to get some work done. When he and Helen had first considered winters in Florida, he had been worried about making ends meet. They had almost given up the whole idea when their oldest son, Matt, introduced them to a promising idea: home-sharing.

"Your house here is so close to the airport," he'd explained. "Do you know how many people from out of town would kill to stay here before a 6 a.m. flight? Or how nice it would be to come someplace like this if you had a long stopover? Much better than a hotel."

At first, Alex and Helen had been skeptical about having strangers stay in their house. Still, they looked into it and soon found that the extra income might be well worth it. They'd soon come to an agreement with their younger son, Blake, who lived in the area and worked as a freelancer: Alex and Helen would take care of all the admin work, and Blake would get the keys to the guests and ensure the house was tidy after check-out. Once a month, Helen would arrange for a cleaning lady to come in. Alex had wanted to give Blake a cut of the profits for his efforts, but his son had insisted that this was unnecessary.

"Dad, give me a break," Blake had said, practically rolling his eyes. "I have two *degrees* because of you. I think I can pop by the house once in a while if it means you can, you know, *breathe* during the winter. Kind of important."

Between their pensions, the home-sharing income, and the few tutoring students Alex had taken on in Florida, the couple was comfortably paying off the remainder of their mortgage in addition to the rent on their new place—and all while living a lifestyle that included Tuesday morning crepes and daily walks in the fresh air.

Identity

SYSTEMIC PERSPECTIVE

More than a Cohort

Understanding the current state.

"I'm working on my life story. I'm not decided if it's going to be a musical or a movie with music in it."

Dolly Parton, Songwriter
and Businessperson,
Interview with Talkshow
Host Alan Titchmarsh

In the past, people often categorized older adults according to age bracket. The idea that the aging population entered "the third age"—that is, retirement—then gained popularity. This third age would naturally follow a fulfilling career, itself preceded by a rambunctious youth. Today, in response to further increases in life expectancy, talks of a "fourth age" are emerging. The fourth age describes the life experiences of aging adults past retirement age, typically those in their seventies, eighties, and beyond.

These attempts to categorize the elderly are inherently ageist, as they rely on stereotypes of people who are—or should be—in decline and losing capacity, desire, time, and often hope. It's true that some aging individuals experience decline in their physical and mental capacities, and that this can also coincide with a loss in desire and hope, but these changes are not experienced by everyone in the same way or at the same time. To understand the experience of aging, we must ask ourselves: What are some of the complex thoughts and feelings associated with the process of aging, and how can we support older adults in navigating these changes while maintaining their sense of self? To answer this question, it's important to move beyond thinking about decline. Instead, we must consider how older adults navigate personal and intellectual growth; how they continue to assess and reassess their understanding of everything, from sexuality to death; and how they navigate their relationships with friends, family, and the world around them.

The Life-Course Approach

An interesting and useful way to think about older adults—and one that is more in keeping with their own self-image and history—is to take the life-course approach. This approach is used to trace a series of events in a person's life, recognizing the relationship between one's sense of self and the social, economic, cultural, and political contexts in which they live.

The life-course approach starts with recognizing, for example, that the 88-year-old woman standing in front of you has experience that goes far beyond her current abilities and life expectancy. She has had a full life, which has been influenced by all of her experiences—both positive and negative. A rich or poor family environment, a short or long formal education, good or not-so-good relationships, a healthy diet or a drug addiction, many social interactions or social isolation, good housing or bad—all of these factors, and many more, have made this person who she is today: Someone shaped by the richness of her unique experiences.

When seen in this light, it becomes clear that this older person is more than just an 88-year-old with poor eyesight and mobility issues. She is a person who has accumulated her own set of knowledge, attitudes, beliefs, and behaviors, all of which influence how she perceives the world, and how the world perceives her. The life-course approach focuses on strengths rather than deficits and losses, and it provides a platform for imagining new and inclusive ways we can all age.

To understand the experience of aging, we
must ask ourselves: What are some of the
complex thoughts and feelings associated
with the process of aging, and how can we
support older adults in navigating these
changes while maintaining their sense of self?

History and Experience

Today's older adults have experienced massive upheavals in human society. They have seen, or even personally experienced, major events that have had significant impacts on individuals and community groups. During their lifetimes, wars and genocides have forever altered the fabric of entire countries and societies; meanwhile, social movements—including those advocating civil rights, gender equality, and sexual freedom—have enabled people to live their lives in new ways. These changes have all been accompanied by unprecedented increases in average and absolute wealth, as well as enormous advances in technology.

Having experienced this relentless pace of change, many older adults have developed the resilience to press on, as well as the knowledge, skills, and intuitive capacities to integrate their experiences into their daily lives. But while these accumulated experiences are essential to the process of understanding and accepting change, we often fail to consider the value of experience as a profoundly useful resource when we think about older adults.

If accumulated experiences—what some would call wisdom—were given the recognition they deserve, we might realize that we can learn something from those who have lived through decades of large-scale transitions and long-term relationships. Older adults have something to teach us about the upheavals of the present and the tools we might use to mitigate stress, and they might even help us gain the perspective needed to create meaning and context around our predictions for the future.

In this chapter, we will explore how aging can be viewed from a different lens, both inter- and intra-personally, as well as how ageism enforces a false narrative regarding the elderly that is highly damaging to society as a whole.

The Experience of Forming or Reforming one's Identity in Later Life

Exploring the context of self-expression.

"Anyone who has been immersed in anthropology is doomed to be an insider-outside for the rest of their life; they can never take anything entirely at face value, but are compelled to constantly ask: why?"

Gillian Tett, Author and Journalist, *The Silo Effect: The Peril of Expertise and the Promise of Breaking Down Barriers*

The ways in which people experience their lives from childhood through to older adulthood are heavily determined by their historical and geographic contexts. While people can express their individual agency in many ways, the manner in which a person develops and moves through their own life is largely shaped by social institutions, such as schools, clinics, community or religious organizations, and political and legislative offices. These are places where rules and regulations are made, and they are also places where cultural norms are reflected and perpetuated.

Older adults living in North America today have all lived through major cultural shifts, but they have experienced those changes differently. Identity markers—including race, gender, ability, immigration status, and others—intersect with age to powerfully shape each individual's experiences, which in turn impact each person's understanding of their own identity.

In this chapter, we examine what it means to be an older adult, focusing on the relationship between societal expectations on the one hand, and subjective experiences of life on the other. The analysis is underpinned by the understanding that although each individual's experience of aging is unique, older adults in specific contexts are likely to have overlapping experiences. We provide an overview of important cultural phenomena that shape how people respond to prevailing notions about how older adults ought to look, think, feel, and behave as they age. This analysis enables us to more clearly imagine how emergent forces of change will generate new cultural norms, thereby influencing what it means to age in the future.

Influence +
Control

Over the course of a lifetime, people continuously define and redefine themselves in relation to others. Each individual develops a sense of self by expressing their own characteristics and beliefs while simultaneously observing the impact their actions have on other people. Expressions of self rely on imagination, sense-making, and storytelling; they often involve developing a coherent narrative, one that allows the individual to purposefully organize the disparate details that comprise their identity.

The process of aging has a profound effect on an individual's sense of self, not only because of the physical effects of aging, but also because age impacts how an individual feels about where they belong, and about their purpose in life. As an individual develops new interests, opinions, capabilities, and world views, the narrative that they previously developed about their identity may become outdated. For those individuals with changing cognitive abilities, old stories may also become fragmented or altered entirely.

The process of aging has a profound effect on an individual's sense of self, not only because of the physical effects of aging, but also because age impacts how an individual feels about where they belong, and about their purpose in life.

Despite the potential disorienting effects of aging on a person's established sense of self, there is a growing resistance to the notion that changes in ability, function, or social role should result in a loss of one's ability to actively construct one's own selfhood. Many older adults are challenging cultural expectations that aging makes one senile, confused, or less of a person; instead, these individuals are choosing to overtly embrace the unique opportunity that aging offers to reinvent the self.

"**Research and theory indicate that cognition is an adaptive process and elders who practice learning activities will maintain their abilities. Further, research and theory of the psychological state of older adults suggest that reminiscence or 'life review' is of serious consequence.**"

Mary Alice Wolf, Gerontology Professor, "Selfhood and the Older Learner: The Promise of Education," from a paper presented at the 1987 Meeting of the American Association for Adult and Continuing Education

Stereotypes +
Ageism

Although many people try to avoid judging others based on preconceived ideas about social groups, the pervasiveness of stereotypes make such resistance challenging. Because it relies on heuristics and taken-for-granted assumptions, the act of stereotyping is often invisible—making it as much a contributor to oppression and discrimination as the most explicit forms of prejudice and bigotry.

Stereotypes about older adults are particularly difficult to avoid, as North American popular culture is rife with references to what it means to be older. The message delivered across markets—evident in everything from birthday cards, to sitcoms, to advertisements for anti-aging products—is that aging means loss. Loss of relevance, of contribution, of capacity to engage with others, and, of course, of personal traits like memory, beauty, and mobility. The stereotypes perpetuated about older adults fuel the normalization and institutionalization of age-based

discrimination, also called ageism.

Ageism explains many of the ways that older adults experience the world—such as how they are sometimes passed over for promotions or pushed out of the workplace entirely, or how their concerns are often dismissed by healthcare professionals. Ageism also intersects in significant ways with other forms of discrimination, such as racism and sexism, resulting in a greater impact for certain sub-populations of older adults.

There are also some positive stereotypes about older people, perhaps the most common being the assumption that seniors have accumulated wisdom over their lifetime. However, many older people resist those as well. Just like their younger peers, many seniors are uncomfortable with any assumption that reduces their individual experiences to a simplified, age-based generalization.

"Most people believe age discrimination begins when workers hit their 50s, according to AARP research of workers between the ages of 45 and 74. Still, 22% believe it begins even earlier, when workers hit their 30s and 40s."

Kimberly Palmer, Author, "10 Things You Should Know About Age Discrimination," AARP

Leadership

Many companies, political associations, and social organizations choose young people as their leaders. This is based on the assumption that only those under the age of 50 can anticipate the needs and wants of the next generations, and these younger leaders are therefore more capable of attracting revenue, votes, or committed membership. This type of thinking is in line with the idea that leadership is the ability to be assertive, in touch with current norms, and/or able to imagine future states.

When older people are chosen as leaders, they are asked to adopt or at least demonstrate the qualities of their younger colleagues. If their knowledge and experience are valued, this often needs to be balanced with the tone, culture, and overall busy nature of contemporary work environments. In the corporate world, for example, retired professionals sometimes assume positions that enable them to impress their ideas and insights on different decision-making processes. These opportunities, however, are unevenly distributed among older adults, and—mirroring other instances of privilege—are disproportionately accessed by seniors who are wealthy, white, and male.

Whereas former professionals hold

Older adults who did not have professional careers face greater challenges when it comes to sharing their wisdom, skills, or passions.

power through advisory roles, as board directors, or as volunteers, older adults who did not have professional careers face greater challenges when it comes to sharing their wisdom, skills, or passions. It is no coincidence that the same groups who are less likely to have had professional careers, including women and people of color, are also rarely found in formal positions of power later in life.

"The term Elder refers to someone who has attained a high degree of understanding of First Nation, Métis, or Inuit history, traditional teachings, ceremonies, and healing practices. Elders have earned the right to pass this knowledge on to others and to give advice and guidance on personal issues, as well as on issues affecting their communities and nations. First Nation, Métis, and Inuit peoples value their Elders and all older people, and address them with the utmost respect."

Dr. Nicole Bell, "Deepening Knowledge: Resources For and About Aboriginal Education," *University of Toronto*

Carrie's Story

Bringing to life current challenges in identity.

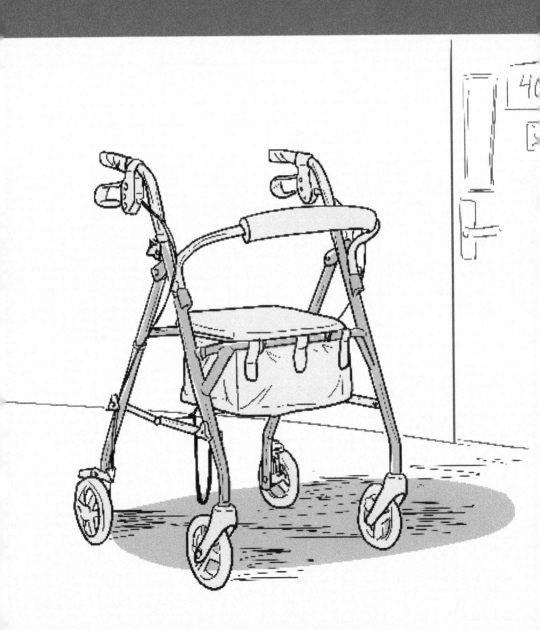

To help bring to life the concepts explored throughout this book, we have created personas for each chapter. A persona grounds ethnographic research within an individual narrative and reveals how overarching themes may play out for a particular person.

The persona for this chapter is Carrie, whose story is intended to embody insights about how aging adults cope with challenges related to changes in identity. Here, we look at how the challenges discussed so far in this chapter may manifest in Carrie's life. At the end of the chapter, we will see another version of Carrie's story: one in which some of the possibilities discussed throughout this chapter have been enacted, resulting in a positive environment that supports Carrie as her identity grows and changes with age.

Carrie is in her late seventies. Due to complications of heart disease, she lives in a nursing home where she receives support with tasks of daily living. She has a younger brother, Malcolm, who is 10 years her junior. Carrie struggles to connect with the other residents of her nursing home, and she spends a great deal of time reflecting on her past. Though her passion is music, Carrie had a successful career as a hotel manager. Now that she is retired, dependent on the care of others, and socially isolated, Carrie is struggling to discover what truly makes her happy.

The story below represents a brief glimpse into Carrie's daily life, including the challenges she faces around shaping her identity to fit her changing life circumstances.

Carrie looked out at the highway from the bench where she sat. Although her legs felt heavier each day, she still tried to make it outside in the mornings—otherwise, she would end up spending the entire day alone in her bedroom.

She often thought about how much time she spent just sitting around these days, waiting for the hours to pass. For decades, she had spent her days bustling about a busy hotel, making sure everything was in order. There had been days where she'd forgotten to eat lunch, days when she got into her car and realized she hadn't sat down in 10 hours. Now, just walking outside to the bench by the door of the nursing home was a great effort.

The touch of someone's hand on her shoulder startled her. "Carrie, how are you feeling?" It was Shira, one of Carrie's least favorite nurses. "Would you like to start heading back soon?" Shira asked in her usual high-pitched, condescending tone. Carrie nodded.

Shira grabbed Carrie's walker, which she'd left beside the bench, and placed it in front of Carrie as she slowly stood. She felt a familiar sense of tension rising in her chest as she switched positions—a feeling she had gotten used to over the past couple of years.

"So, what's the plan for today, Miss Carrie?" Shira asked as she and Carrie made their way to the door. "I hear that Cameron is going to be playing something for us this afternoon. Would you like to come into the common room to listen?"

"That piano is out of tune," Carrie said, her voice sharp. "I've been telling you that since I moved here. Two years that thing has been out of tune, and it's only getting worse."

Shira quickly brushed this off. "Oh, I think it sounds alright. But if you're not in the mood for music, that's OK. You can visit with your friends this evening at movie night instead. I'll leave a note for Lisa to come get you at 6:30 so that you have lots of time to make it before they start playing the film at 7:00. I think they're showing American Graffiti. Doesn't that sound fun?"

That afternoon, Carrie sat in her recliner with the TV on, daydreaming. It felt good to have her legs up like this. She closed her eyes and imagined she was sunbathing on a beach lounge chair, just like she'd done so often when she was young. Back then, her body had been strong and reliable. Her legs had taken her wherever she wanted to go—she and her friends had even traveled across the country, playing shows in dingy local bars along the way to pay for gas and food.

That had been before everything changed—before her mother suddenly passed away, and before she found herself the sole provider and caregiver for her younger brother, Malcolm, who was barely 13. The responsibility had forced her to grow up quickly, and now here she was, an old woman being treated like a child. The irony was almost too much to bear.

A light tap on the door broke her reverie. She opened her eyes just as the door opened a crack.

"Carrie? Are you decent?" The deep voice was a familiar one.

"Come in, Malcolm."

Her brother entered the room and closed the door behind him. As he came closer to where Carrie sat, she noticed how distinguished he looked in his navy blue blazer and thick-rimmed frames. He leaned over to give her a kiss on the cheek, then settled on the couch across from her.

"You look handsome," Carrie said, smiling. "No court today?"

"No, but I just finished teaching a class at the university. I thought I would drop by for a quick visit." Malcolm coughed lightly into the crook of his elbow. "Hope I'm not interrupting anything."

Over the next half hour, Carrie listened attentively as her younger brother told her all about his life. He talked about the latest drama going on with his university faculty, and about the most interesting cases his firm was working on. She smiled with genuine delight as he told stories about his children and grandchildren. Before Carrie knew it, he was heading for the door.

"I'll come back as soon as I can," Malcolm said after kissing her once more on the cheek.

"Bring the kids next time. It's been too long since they've visited their aunt Carrie," she said.

Just as quickly as he'd come in, Malcolm was gone. The TV droned quietly on in the background as Carrie leaned back and closed her eyes once more, trying not to think about how much she envied the little brother she had raised.

Transforming How We See Ourselves Through Age

The future of identifying as old(er).

"With age comes acumen. With experience comes insight."

Chris Bohjalian,
Novelist, from
Secrets of Eden

To understand how the aging population will come to redefine identity, it is important to first identify and articulate "shifts"—that is, large-scale transitions that are taking place within society today. Throughout this book, we use these shifts to help articulate the tensions that emerged during our foresight research. We performed diverse scanning of various moments of change influencing Western society, whether those came in the form of a film, article, tech startups, or conversation. Shifts allow us to frame new questions and establish future-oriented points of view, enabling us to imagine and create more meaningful realities for aging individuals.

SHIFT 1

From Reflecting

to Reinventing Ourselves

Having the space and opportunity to experiment with self-expression increases health and resilience. People can continue to re-shape themselves and re-create their life stories as they age.

"I keep thinking there must have been something that a real man could have done about it. Something short of guns, but more effective than Oil of Olay. But I failed. I did nothing. I absolutely failed to stay young."

Ursula K. Le Guin, Author, from *The Waves in the Mind*

> Resilience Through Change

Later life is commonly seen as a time for reflection, a time defined by stability rather than disruption. But older adults also experience unexpected events—such as a life crisis, a cancer diagnosis, a stroke, the loss of a spouse or employment income, or the inability to do the things that give them joy—that interrupt the stability of later life. If, after a period of grieving, an individual is unable to integrate or make sense of such an experience, then they may begin to dwell on the past or otherwise let the crisis define them, making it difficult to live in the present or to move forward.

66

"Most forms of psychotherapy have emphasized the therapeutic effects of disclosure in order to come to terms with traumatic or highly stressful events. Freud believed that only through vocal expression could one truly gain perspective into one's own psyche. Suppression of self-expression seems to be connected to mental illness and psychopathology. It has also been related to negative stress responses and to many physical problems, such as coronary heart disease."

Heejung S. Kim and Deborah Ko, "Culture and Self-Expression," *Frontiers of Social Psychology: The Self*

Comfortable Routines, Not New Dreams

A life crisis is an event that usually forces a person to change. An individual may experience a situational crisis, such as a cancer diagnosis or the death of a partner; a developmental crisis, such as the end of one's child-rearing days; or even an existential crisis, which might lead to a re-evaluation of one's life purpose. Regardless of the nature of the change, finding the time or space to reimagine one's life after a crisis can make life more meaningful. This type of disruption can be an opportunity for reinvention and transformation.

Two areas in which older adults choose to re-imagine their futures are in their relationships and careers. While divorce rates peaked around 1980, among older adults, they have continued to rise dramatically.

Increased longevity is leading many seniors to question whether their marriages of 40 or 50 years are still affirming. While some individuals—particularly heterosexual women—choose to leave their marriages to focus on self-care, others ask instead how to find fulfillment through work. For some, this might mean mentoring younger employees, while others choose to pursue "encore" careers or entrepreneurship. Self-employment among those of retirement age is rising. In the US, 4.5 million Americans aged 50–70 are engaged in an encore career, and another 31 million wish they had one.

Older adults are also reinventing themselves in less dramatic ways. For example, many choose to downsize to smaller homes, or to move in order to be closer to their grandchildren. Others are realizing that they find purpose in and take pleasure from volunteering, traveling, or taking classes to learn new skills. This openness to exploration and experimentation is vital to health and well-being, at any age.

Increased longevity is leading many seniors to question whether their marriages of 40 or 50 years are still affirming.

SIGNALS

#1

Adulthood Two

In her book *Composing a Life*, anthropologist Mary Catherine Bateson posits that one positive aspect of increased longevity is that it gives rise to a second stage that she terms "active adulthood." Unlike the first stage of adulthood, where people are preoccupied with raising children or building careers, this stage is an opportunity for greater engagement with the world and more reflection on questions surrounding what makes work satisfying and worthwhile, what it means to be married, or how to find a spiritual practice. Whereas earlier in life people tend to react to life's circumstances, Bateson believes that people become more intentional later in life. She sees an opportunity for people in this life phase to approach aging as one might approach the creation of a story or art piece: by composing different pieces in the pursuit of new meaning.

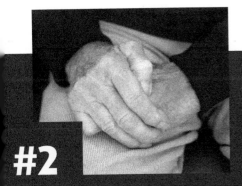

#2

Trauma Informed Care

The Adverse Childhood Experiences (ACE) questionnaire was designed in the 1990s to help assess the long-term health impacts of traumatic childhood events. While the study used to develop this test focused on children, newer studies looking at older adults show that those who experience a traumatic event later in life exhibit behaviors similar to those of younger adults who have experienced trauma, including hostility, social isolation, and agitation. Additionally, people who have experienced trauma in the distant past are more likely to have difficulties with memory, sleep problems, and loss of appetite.

However, few health professionals assess for or even understand the role of trauma in the lives of older adults, and some may even dismiss these symptoms as a normal part of aging. Several tools, including the Life Events Checklist and the Traumatic Life Events Questionnaire, have been designed to address this gap. The latter is an adult screening tool that was recently developed to help health professionals learn about a person's trauma, if any, and to facilitate a trauma-informed approach to care. The tool helps HCPs identify certain life stressors that may have impacted an individual across their lifespan. Acknowledging past traumas could be an important first step toward helping individuals leave the trauma behind, heal, and re-engage with life.

SHIFT 2
From Accumulating Knowledge

In a "trending" world, wisdom
is becoming less about what one
knows and more about fostering a
deep connection over a long period
of time.

"Highly generative people—
that is, people who are caring
and committed to helping
future generations—often
tell stories about others who
helped them in the past."

Brady K. Jones and Dan P.
McAdams, "Becoming Generative:
Socializing Influences Recalled in
Life Stories in Late Midlife,"
The Journal of Adult Development

to Becoming a Wise Leader

Experience as Currency

As noted earlier, older adults have long been associated with a type of wisdom that their younger counterparts often rely on for advice and guidance. This continues to be the case in a number of cultures, where the accumulated knowledge, experiences, and mistakes that make up a long life are revered and respected. While this perspective has not always been present in wealthy Western nations, recently, recognition of the lived experiences of older adults has been increasing. One example can be seen in the growing popularity of celebrities who are embracing aging and resisting pressure to maintain a youthful persona. In the last five years, there

Older adults who did not have professional careers face greater challenges when it comes to sharing their wisdom, skills, or passions.

has been an increase in the use of older adults as models for women's clothing—whether it be Joan Didion for Celine, Joni Mitchell for Saint Laurent, Vivienne Westwood's collaboration with Burberry, or the countless other older models being used in runway shows, such as Lauren Hutton and Maye Musk. Influenced by a myriad of variables, this trend may represent a tipping point in postmodern feminism, in which women are resisting the long-term objectification that has long taken the guise—particularly in the fashion industry—as a form of empowerment. This pursuit of an aesthetic that goes beyond what is "hot" or "beautiful" may be a sign that the fashion industry is beginning to understand that age—and the years of adventure it represents—might be more sell-worthy than sex.

"If you are wise… you're not going to focus so much on what you need and deserve, but on what you can contribute."

Laura L. Carstensen, as quoted by Phyllis Korkki in "The Science of Older and Wiser," *The New York Times*

From Building Capabilities to Teaching Cooperation

In today's digital world, in which information is more accessible than ever before, the answers to life's problems are often just a click away. However, when it comes to benefiting from wise counsel, it is important not to confuse expert knowledge with wisdom.

Those researching the concept of wisdom are working to understand how one becomes wise and what it means to lead wisely. Columbia University professor Ursula Staudinger, for example, suggests that wise leaders are those who take time for reflection, learn from their experiences,

and use their insights to solve problems and help others. Otto Scharmer, an innovator in organizational change methods at MIT, has similar thoughts: "It is not *what* leaders do or *how* they do it, but rather the *inner place* from which they operate," he explains, "It is the quality of awareness and consciousness leaders bring to a situation." In other words, wisdom is less about what one knows and more about who one is. Wise leaders are those who work on themselves in order to authentically support others.

Self-reflection and generosity toward others are not only behaviors central to thoughtful leadership—they are also behaviors that are more likely to develop as people age. Years ago, Carl Jung often discussed this idea in his writings and with his students, but more recent research is adding further depth to our understanding of why people may become more thoughtful and engaged as they age. A recent article in *Topics in*

Wisdom is less about what one knows and more about who one is.

Cognitive, an academic journal, points out that older people actually have more information in their brains than younger people, not less. This pushes against the myth of cognitive decline, and adds credence to theories that position aging as a process of becoming. Such theories suggest that as people age, they become less driven by self interest and more interested, as Phyllis Korkki suggests in an article for *The New York Times*, in the bigger social, cultural, and political picture. This shift may also lead them to become more open to serving others. Key to research on this topic is the insight that although older people take longer to process information, they address matters that are important to them in more sensitive, nuanced ways.

If it's true that nurturing behavior is associated with aging, organizations looking to improve their leadership capabilities should make space for older employees—particularly those committed to creating positive change. Rather than giving seniors the golden handshake, organizations might create new positions that allow those approaching retirement age to continue to contribute in new ways—as mentors, for example. Mentoring means providing guidance in a way that requires the humility to listen, ask questions, and build relationships based on curiosity and interest in who the mentee is and can become—something far more significant than merely what they can accomplish. This can also include reverse mentoring, in which an older adult is mentored by someone younger. This can be especially rewarding when the younger person is someone from a different cultural, social, or economic background than that of the older adult

SIGNALS

#1

Meaningful Relationships

In the business world, people often attribute their skill-building to influential mentors who have helped them by asking the right questions. This relationship benefits not only mentees, but also mentors, as they're given time to develop and model the compassion that's required to offer relevant advice, and to further reflect on and articulate their own experiences and insights. Companies are recognizing that when they choose to create a culture of development in the workplace, older employees gain the opportunity to help their less experienced co-workers succeed in both work and life. This can make business relationships more meaningful and productive. The CSARN Mentorship Program in Ontario pairs senior artists with younger artists, giving both the opportunity to share and learn. The program places an emphasis on the unique experiences of older artists who have worked in different time periods and with unique media, which adds depth to these interactions. Mentors have to be 60 years of age or older, with at least 20 years of experience as an artist. Mentors are even paid for their time, so the program also operates as a part-time employment opportunity.

#2

Intuitive Leadership

The lack of people willing to take responsibility for decisions is a pervasive problem in many organizations today. Some speculate that today's leaders find it difficult to feel confident in their own intuition when they're overwhelmed by data. However, some business leaders—like Shelley Row, MBA and author of *Think Less Live More: Lessons from a Recovering Over-Thinker*—are increasingly talking about leveraging intuition when faced with big decisions. That intuition, in line with our common understanding of wisdom, develops and expands with every new experience. Recognizing the value of experienced leaders, Revera, a provider of housing and care for seniors in Canada, appointed the former mayor of Mississauga, Ontario, Hazel McCallion, as their Chief Elder Officer (the "other" CEO). In this role, 98-year-old McCallion draws on her many decades of political experience to counsel Revera.

SHIFT 3

From Avoiding Mortality

to Increasing Agency Over End-of-Life Experiences

The desire to die on one's own terms often refers to a decision to end medical intervention. Those ready to end attempts to prolong life often imagine dying at home surrounded by their loved ones. Inherent to dying on one's own terms is focusing on each individual's end-of-life journey—in large part by honoring the life that preceded that final stage.

66

"My own experience of aging is [that] there are capacities I had ten years ago [that] I no longer have, and I have to reflect upon those losses and the loss that all of us will face in anticipation of death. It is something that brings great depth and meaning into our lives and also helps us to articulate, internally, our priorities— what is really important for us."

Joan Halifax, Zen Buddhist teacher and author, excerpt from interview with the *On Being* podcast

> Death, Reimagined

In North America, fear around death and dying often manifests as a quest for longer life. Interest in life-extending and death-preventing technologies continues to grow, with many biotech companies attempting to capitalize on the collective fear of death by encouraging consumers to pursue life extension through anti-aging interventions, regenerative medicine, cryopreservation, and even digital immortality. However, while Silicon Valley fantasizes about curing aging and even escaping death, death remains as natural a part of life as birth. Today, people are becoming more open to talking about what has long been a taboo topic. They are discovering that speaking about death is not only an opportunity to explore their fears and goals for their remaining years, but also to ask important questions about what makes life meaningful and enjoyable.

"Some may want to participate in planning rituals before or after death. In some religious traditions, confession of sins, preparation to 'meet one's maker,' or asking forgiveness from those who may have been wronged can be part of end-of-life concerns. In other cultural traditions, planning or even discussing death is considered inappropriate, uncaring, and even dangerous, as it is viewed as inviting death."

American Psychological Association, *End of Life Issues and Care*

Courageous Acceptance, Not Avoidance of Death

Attitudes toward death are changing, and it is becoming increasingly normal for people to think about and openly discuss death, even in public forums. In their respective books, *Being Mortal* and *A Good Death: Making the Most of our Final Choices*, Dr. Atul Gawande and Dr. Sandra Martin urge people to talk about death with their doctors, and with each other. Gawande writes, "We pay doctors to give chemotherapy and to do surgery, but not to take the time required to sort out when to do so is unwise." Both authors believe that once people are made aware of their options and given time to consider their values and goals, they will be empowered to initiate these difficult conversations with their healthcare providers. As Martin argues in her work, "Prolonged lifespans and crippling medical bills... necessitate a new branch of civil liberty, one where we choose our own death and those choices are respected." These books represent a larger attempt to shift medicine away from the goal of simply increasing lifespan regardless of the human and healthcare costs, and instead toward a consideration of each individual's priorities in life and end-of-life needs.

People are beginning to have more open conversations not only about how and where they want to die, but also regarding when they might want to die.

With the recent legalization of assisted dying in a number of countries, including Canada and some US states, people are beginning to have more open conversations not only about how and where they want to die, but also regarding when they might want to die. There are even some extreme examples of this thinking; take, for example, 61-year-old Ezekiel Emanuel, an oncologist and Director of Bioethics at the US National Institutes of Health (NIH). In his controversial article for *The Atlantic*, "Why I Hope to Die at 75," Emanuel states that 75 is the ideal time to die because, as he sees it, it's the age at which one can claim to have lived a full life. As he puts it, "Why would one run the risk of dementia, drooling, and being a burden to one's family?"

While many would argue that Emanuel's logic itself is the result of stereotyping about older adults, he is a significant figure, and he is not alone in his desire to dictate the terms of his own death. When responding to surveys asking whether they would choose to live with a serious illness or in a state that affects their independence—such as living with dementia, being bedridden, or being reliant on a ventilator—the majority of respondents said that they would prefer an earlier death.

While the healthcare system has a responsibility to respect patients' end-of-life wishes, it is also obligated to ensure that those in their final years understand all of their options. People with serious illnesses shouldn't feel that they are a burden, nor

While the healthcare system has a responsibility to respect patients' end-of-life wishes, it is also obligated to ensure that those in their final years understand all of their options.

should they believe that medical assistance in dying is the only rational solution for coping with their declining physical and mental abilities. The desire for death among the elderly, while often the result of unbearable pain and suffering, might also be in response to inadequate end-of-life options resulting from the ageism inherent to healthcare and other public services. As Dr. Elizabeth Dzeng observes, "It's a small step from feeling invisible or unwanted to wanting to physically vanish." While there are options for prolonging one's life, as well as options for ending one's life, what is often lacking is care that truly supports and prepares one for death.

SIGNALS

#1

Death Care

Tired of highly institutionalized and commercialized funeral rites, some people are seeking more intimate rituals that allow them to approach dying with a sense of meaning and vulnerability. Capsula Mundi is a design concept for eco-friendly burial pods made from biodegradable materials. A tree of one's choosing is planted over the pod, and nutrients from the decomposing body act as fertilizer for the tree. There are also some people looking to add a performative flare to their deaths. These individuals are opting to have parties, shows, or other events instead of traditional funerals. An interesting example is that of 28-year-old Andrew Henderson of Manitoba, Canada. After learning that he had terminal cancer, Henderson decided to star in his own funeral, and to use the event as a way to confront the way we think and talk about death. Henderson produced "Taking it to the Grave," a performance piece complete with confessions, taboos, and Henderson seated inside a champagne bottle, just days before his death.

#2

Death Positivity

By discussing death with other people, friends and strangers alike, individuals can strengthen their social bonds with others and gain greater empathy, all while exploring end-of-life issues. Building on this insight, the non-profit Death Over Dinner facilitates shared dinners during which diners are encouraged to discuss death. Similarly, death cafes and festivals of death and dying have become worldwide phenomena in recent years. These offer a familiar environment where people can come to discuss difficult questions, such as what to say to a friend who is dying, or to contemplate what they might learn from the experience of having a loved one die. These events are sometimes led by "death doulas": companions or coaches who work in the community or in hospice care to support the dying and their families with the practical and emotional aspects of death, such as funeral arrangements, caregiving, or completion of advance care directives.

SHIFT 4

From Conforming

to Authentically Enacting Gender and Sexuality

Older people are increasingly seeing their sexuality and gender as fluid. Being in their later years enables people to reject the stringent expectations surrounding masculinity and femininity, allowing them to reimagine or re-invest in their sexual identities.

"Betty Friedan, who trained as a social psychologist, researched the issue of aging late in her life, and suggested that there is a 'fountain of age,' a period of renewal, growth, and experimentation based on a new freedom."

Linda P. Fried, Columbia University, "Making Aging Positive," *The Atlantic*

> Radical Tolerance

Affirmative aging is about more than just
"being active." It's about having agency and
acknowledging—and then taking control
of—one's needs, wants, and identity formation. In an article in *The International
Journal of Aging and Later Life*, social work
researcher Linn Sandberg argues for an
"affirmative old age as an alternative concep-
tualization of old age"—one that works
against the binary concepts of decline and
success, instead reframing what it means
to live well through the aging process.
Affirmative aging has long been discussed in
academic and popular literature. It is viewed
as an active approach to one's identity—
something that is important across many
aspects of life, including the realm of gender
and sexuality.

Affirmative aging acknowledges that
rigid definitions of what constitutes socially
acceptable behavior for people over 50
remain. Many women, in particular, feel the
need (both real and imagined) to conform
to societal expectations and to remain sexually desirable in ways associated with youth;
otherwise, they may risk losing a spouse
or career. Social workers Jill Chonody and
Barbra Teater attribute this to mytholog-
ical qualities of how people think about

aging. As they put it in their book, *Social
Work Practice With Older Adults*, "Aging
myths, which form the basis for stereotypes,
create a limited social perspective on older
people, and, as a consequence, older people
are thought of and treated as if they 'all the
same'." Yet, these stereotypes bear cultural
specificity: Older adults are lumped together
in different ways across different times and
places.

For example, today's older North
American women are living in a time and

The idea that one must be either youthful and sexual or old-looking and desire-less is being replaced by the understanding that gender and sexuality can be as fluid for an older person as it is for a teenager.

place when the norms associated with gender roles and sexual identities are truly being challenged, both in mainstream culture and in small social pockets that are increasingly accessible to people of all ages and backgrounds. Women are resisting what cultural critic Laura Kipnis calls a "feminine industrial complex": that is, the pressure to spend time and money on expensive interventions, like botox and tummy tucks, to obtain physically perfected bodies. As older women continue to embrace their evolving aesthetics and senses of self, the image of what it means to be an older person is also changing. The idea that one must be either youthful and sexual or old-looking and desire-less is being replaced by the understanding that gender and sexuality can be as fluid for an older person as it is for a teenager.

"Changing sexual scripts can potentially contribute to decreased gender inequity in the sexual realm and to increased opportunities for sexual satisfaction, safety, and well-being, particularly for women, but for men as well."

N. Tatiana Masters, Erin Casey, Elizabeth A. Wells, and Diane M. Morrison, "Sexual Scripts Among Young Heterosexually Active Men and Women: Continuity and Change," *Journal of Sex Research*

From Submission to Self-Expression

As people get older, they become more likely to prioritize authentic self-expression over traditional gender and sexuality norms. Older women, in particular, are increasingly revisiting their gender roles. They are doing this not in spite of aging, but as a result of it. Finally free of the stringent expectations that were imposed on many of them throughout their reproductive years, these women are re-imagining and re-defining who they are, on their own terms. Some are choosing to embrace the gender- and sex-neutrality available to them in their post-menopausal years, perhaps even taking on the traditionally masculine social and political roles that were less available to them when they were younger. Others are choosing to go in a different direction by enacting their femininity and feminine sexuality in new and newly overt ways. This might mean embracing dramatic fashion trends, blogging about their experiences as older women, or engaging in sex tourism that gives them a sense of power and adventure.

Older men are also using their later years as a time to explore their passions in new ways. Some are rejecting pharmaceutical interventions for erectile dysfunction in favor of natural remedies, while others experiencing natural declines in sex drive are rejecting altogether the notion that sexual activity is a necessary part of their lives. Others are embracing sexuality, often in ways that were previously deemed unsuitable or impractical for men in their social positions. Whether they are coming out, or simply coming into their own, older adults are looking for new experiences that strengthen the connection between their minds and bodies. Inspired perhaps by the approaches their younger peers take to pursue gender fluidity, older adults are no doubt bringing their own sense of power to the process, infusing the movement with a sense of entitlement born of experience and self-awareness.

SIGNALS

#1

Sex + Aging

Older adults face a lot of difficulties when it comes to openly discussing sexuality, because society is still uncomfortable with the idea of sexuality in older people—especially in older women. Many people assume that older women are not interested in sex, or that they've become generally asexual, having lost aspects of their sexuality as they've aged. Dr. Holly Thomas, a physician and researcher at the University of Pittsburgh's Department of Medicine, challenges this idea. In her research, she found that almost 60% of women over 60 are sexually active, and that many are just as satisfied with their sex lives as they were in their thirties. Some participants reported having better sex now than when they were younger, partly because they feel more confident, assertive, and able to communicate their needs. Jody Hanson, a 68-year-old writer and former professor, has blogged about her experiences with sex tourism, acknowledging that, while older women are perhaps not typically associated with sex tourism, there are a number of prime vacation destinations that now specifically cater to older women looking for holiday romance.

#2

Inclusive Care + Celebration

Though there have been promising signs of greater inclusion for the LGBTQ+ community across Western countries, exclusion is still a common experience for older members of this community. This is especially pronounced for those entering care facilities. Wary of their new living environments, seniors who identify as members of the LGBTQ+ community often feel forced to repress or conceal their sexual identities or orientations when they enter these facilities. To help address these fears, Rainbow Health Ontario, which works to promote the health of Ontario's LGBTQ+ community, trains staff in care homes to provide inclusive care. Their aim is to make LGBTQ+ seniors and couples feel more comfortable expressing their affection for each other, and to make staff more conscious of the legacy of fear and prejudice that many LGBTQ+ seniors still feel. In Australia, a similar initiative called the annual Coming Back Out Ball also addresses these concerns. Rather than a training program, the event serves as a celebration of the resilience of LGBTQ+ and Intersex elders. The Coming Back Out Ball is so named because one of the biggest challenges older people within the LGBTQ+ community face is deciding whether they should be out in late life or keep this aspect of themselves hidden. For seniors who are coming (back) out, including those who have been marginalized and mistreated for their sexual identity or orientation, the Coming Back Out Ball is intended to provide the gift of visibility in a safe, welcoming space.

Bringing to Life the Future of Identity for Older Adults

Building out possible concepts and solutions.

"...critical gerontology offers a lens through which to interpret my personal journey from a core feminist identity to a questioning and ambivalent identity as an old woman."

Margaret Cruikshank, Feminist Writer and Academic, "Aging and Identity Politics," *Journal of Aging Studies*

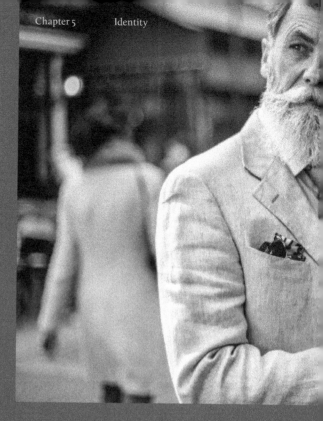

As social and political values continue to evolve, so too does our understanding of the role of identity in later life. By questioning norms around age and examining the feelings of "otherness" that seniors experience, we can transform how older adults like Carrie (the persona for this chapter) experience aging in the future—particularly when it comes to their sense of identity. Regardless of the shifts that take place in technology, economics, and beyond, the human need to organize oneself intrapersonally, and to improve one's understanding of the mind, body, and soul, will remain. Many older adults will continue to reinvent and recalibrate how they express themselves in harmony with changing circumstances, a practice that is often associated with more creatively oriented personalities. On the other hand, many others will struggle to redefine themselves or to find new forms of personal satisfaction as they age. To better support the latter group, we must consider the drivers of identity development that are especially relevant for seniors when we collectively envision the ways in which they will want to foster a sense of self as they age.

EXPERIENCE DRIVERS

Forces Influencing How Older Adults Experience Identity

Identity formation and reformation is triggered and influenced by many variables, both internal and external to the individual. This means that identity is both learned and generated uniquely; in order to design for this complexity, we must put the experiences of older adults—including the people, things, and environments comprising these experiences—at the forefront. The experience drivers below summarize key considerations to keep in mind regarding how aging adults understand their personal experience of aging. These drivers provide points of departure to keep in mind as we imagine ways to ease tensions and improve experiences for seniors in the future.

1. Playing Safe

Many older adults want to experiment with their sense of self, but they also fear that this will jeopardize their existing relationships and social roles.

> How might we create or support programs that invite older adults to develop new interests, skills, and worldviews within environments that are familiar and unthreatening?

2. Representation

To challenge the cultural norms and stereotypes that underpin ageism and other forms of discrimination, aging adults require the support of people of all ages.

> How might we require or encourage media or other cultural institutions and initiatives to depict a realistically diverse range of older adults?

3. Remaining Relevant

The act of sharing skills and knowledge is an important part of formal leadership, but there are plenty of other ways that older adults act as mentors or work in less obvious ways to leave their stamp on the world.

> How might people of all ages facilitate the participation of older people in workplaces, recreational spaces, schools, and/or other private and public institutions?

OPPORTUNITY SPACE

Rethinking Identity Formation and Investing in the Right Initiatives

Given the systemic, experiential, and foresight perspectives brought forward in this chapter, as well as the learnings captured in interviews with aging and healthcare experts across North America and Europe, we have defined an opportunity space as a takeaway. Opportunity spaces capture the key thinking and findings uncovered in our research, while informing and inspiring organizations across industries on how to design better futures, in this case, for older adults.

This chapter's opportunity space intends to challenge conventional thinking around how people perceive and express themselves as they grow older.

Invest in Respect

Context

Older people do not want to be lumped together or defined by their age, particularly because such definitions are typically based on misplaced myths and stereotypes. Just like their younger counterparts, aging adults want their personal histories, lived experiences, and their changing sense of self to drive how they are sold products, services, and experiences.

Opportunity Space

Explore opportunities to promote each person's sense of individuality. Create products and services that support aging adults in moulding their own individual identities while also creating positive change in how older adults are perceived by society more broadly.

An emphasis on distinction would allow older adults to identify as unique, empowered individuals who have been shaped by their many historical, social, cultural, and political experiences. This is a powerful concept, one that is often lost in later age.

To be distinct is to own one's deepest thoughts and feelings, and to make those internal aspects of one's self known to others. This is a critical aspect of what it means to build a better future of aging—one that companies across industries should be more thoughtfully engaging with.

Reimagining Carrie's Story

Throughout this final chapter, we explored the current realities and challenges facing older adults in the context of identity, including how older adults see themselves and how society views this group more broadly.

In closing, we want to reimagine Carrie's story to explore the ways in which she might be empowered to embrace—both publicly and privately—her true self. In this version of Carrie's story, social awareness regarding the experience of older adults has improved. Carrie takes advantage of this social shift; she uses technology to leverage her social network, and in doing so, finds a new way to explore and share her story.

Carrie squinted at the computer screen in concentration. Though one of the nurses had helped her enlarge the font size so that she could see clearly, she couldn't break her habit of squinting and leaning in toward the large monitor while she typed.

She finished her sentence, then sat back and took a sip of her tea. Ever since Carrie had started her blog about six months ago, writing had become part of her afternoon routine. She'd first gotten the idea for the blog after a visit with her niece, Camille. They had been chatting about everything from work, to dating, to kids, and Camille had said something that caught Carrie's attention.

"Aunt Carrie, how do you seem to know so much about everything?" She had asked. Though her tone was light, Carrie could tell that her question was a serious one.

"Well, being old is a real help," Carrie had replied dryly.

Camille laughed. "I know, I know. You're always telling me how old you are, but I know other old people who are nothing like you. Like, I swear, you're actually wise beyond your many, many years."

"I always thought your dad had enough wisdom for the both of us," Carrie said. "I mostly just went through life and figured it out as I went along—not like Malcolm, so meticulous with everything. Sometimes I can't even believe that I raised that man."

"No," Camille said, her voice now completely serious. "Don't you sell yourself short like that, Auntie. Dad may be smart, but you made him good."

Camille paused for a moment. "Seriously," she continued. "You should write a book or something."

That offhand comment hit a nerve. Carrie had been spending a lot of time lately thinking about her past, and she was coming to the realization that she'd never actually put herself—her real self—out there. She'd been working closely with the nursing home's self-expression counsellor, Binh, who was helping her think hard about who she was and who she would like to be. Using tools that Carrie had never been exposed to before, like scrapbooking, vision-boarding, and VR, Binh was encouraging Carrie to reflect on her life, past and present. They'd covered a lot of ground, and for the past month, they'd been focusing on the subject of love, relationships, and sexuality—an area that Carrie found particularly difficult to talk about.

During a recent visualization exercise facilitated by VR, Binh had helped Carrie recreate a memory that she had revisited countless times over the decades. In it, she spent the entire night on a beach with her closest friends; a few of them had even fallen asleep holding hands.

"What brings you here?" Binh asked. "What makes this the place where you feel most connected to your romantic, sexual self?"

"I think about that beach a lot," Carrie replied, feeling some regret and sadness. "It's where I met the one that got away."

The experience gave Carrie's blog, a recent project she'd undertaken, a purpose. At first, Carrie had started writing as a hobby. She wrote about conversations that she'd had with Malcolm, Camille, and her other family members. She recorded stories of funny things that had happened at the nursing home—like the time her friend Jean misplaced a bottle of whiskey and thought that someone had gone through her things. The whiskey turned out to be in the cabinet, exactly where it was supposed to be. They had laughed about the whole thing over a stiff drink.

Now, however, the blog was becoming so much more. Carrie had began writing about her past, about what she'd given up when she became Malcolm's primary caregiver. She wrote about the marriage proposal she'd received (and turned down) in her thirties. She wrote—and, in doing so, finally admitted to herself—about the relief she'd always felt when she turned away the men who came knocking over the years. She wrote about how she'd used raising Malcolm as an excuse not to date, when really, the only person she'd ever wanted to spend time with was Audrey— her dearest friend from those wild days on the beach. She wrote:

> I couldn't admit it to myself, but it's so clear to me now. I denied those feelings, but they were always there, and I think Audrey shared them. The truth is, I loved her. No, actually: I was in love with her. These memories roar back now, with a new life, new vigor, new heartache. We lost Audrey years ago, and though it saddens me to know that I will never be able to share my feelings with her, I can't help but feel lucky to finally have accepted and embraced this part of myself. And, of course, to be sharing it with all of you.

She published the stories in small doses, one or two pages a week. The blog was widely read by her friends, family, and residents. It even became part of the self-expression therapy group, with Carrie leading a new initiative on gender and sexual identity.

A few weeks into the blog's new life, Priya, a quiet resident of the home, had approached Carrie at dinner.

"So-so," she stuttered, "You're tell-telling me that no one has proposed to you in about fi-fi-fifty years? I f-find that hard to believe."

"Well, I didn't date very much after that," Carrie said.

Priya looked down at her shoes. She laughed lightly, as though something was amusing her, then looked back up at Carrie. "Never too late to start again," she said.

As Priya walked back to her table, Carrie found herself grinning. She placed her hand over her mouth and stifled a giggle, thinking, *I can't wait to write about this later.*

Conclusion:
A Conversation with
Jeanne Beker

When we began working on *The Future of Aging*, our goal was simple: We wanted to create a resource that would help organizations design better possible futures for aging adults. We spoke to experts across healthcare, innovation, and design; we gathered signals of change to learn everything we could about new approaches to old problems; and we read as many books and articles as possible in order to uncover the many challenges facing the aging population.

Still, we knew that our work was not yet done. After all, how could we call this book complete without including the perspective of someone representing the very group we'd worked so hard to understand and plan for—someone who would be directly affected by the changes we were proposing?

We were thrilled when Canadian icon Jeanne Beker agreed to provide that very perspective. Known best for her long-time role as host of *Fashion Television*, Beker is not only a prolific television personality, but also an experienced writer, editor, and entrepreneur. The fashion journalist is a member of the Order of Canada and an inductee in Canada's Walk of Fame—not to mention an international presence in the fashion industry. At 67 years old, Beker is just beginning to confront some of the challenges we explore in this work, making her the perfect candidate to reflect on how we might build a

better future for aging adults.

We asked Beker what comes to mind when she thinks about growing older. "I've found a wonderful sense of acceptance has come with age, and a creeping awareness that time is of the essence," she explained. Aging has resulted in a stronger sense of self for Beker, and it has granted her the freedom to pursue long-held interests. "I'm finally making and taking time to smell the roses," she said. "Embracing those passions that have always been so important to me—but that sadly often took a backseat to everything else I was busy pursuing—has been a real blessing." Beker also stressed the importance of embracing her vitality by staying active, both physically and mentally, and continuing down the same path of growth she has long walked. "I never think about [aging]," she explained. "I have always remained connected to my 17-year-old self."

Not all individuals are able to maintain such a strong sense of identity as Beker, who described "feeling totally comfortable in one's own skin" as "another brilliant gift that comes with age." However, as we explore in Chapter 5, aging is a time of growth for many. By considering the ways in which individuals like Beker work to live active, fulfilling, and meaningful lives, organizations across industries will be equipped to design products and services that provide aging adults with the agency to achieve their goals. This includes their pursuit of authentic self-expression, which is something Beker feels strongly about—particularly considering her fashion background. "Self-expression is *always* important, in my book," she explained. "It always has been. But with age, there's no need to apologize—at least not as much—so it's important to express oneself to one's own self, and to others you care to leave your mark with." What role, we wondered, does the fashion industry play in facilitating this self-expression? "When it comes to fashion, I'm a firm believer in dressing for one's body type *and* spirit," Beker responded. "Chronological age should not play as big a role in determining what to wear. I also believe that the older we get, the more ourselves we become. So hopefully, being true to yourself becomes a whole a lot easier."

When it comes to reaching such goals and coping with new challenges, Beker stressed the importance of maintaining ties with others: "It's all about community—staying connected with old friends and connecting with new ones." This can mean fostering relationships with other aging adults, but also with people across generations, cultures, and backgrounds. For Beker, a beloved media personality and member of the international fashion community, a sense of belonging is in no short supply. And so, we asked, what challenges *did* she expect to face in the next 20 years, or even in the next 5? "I just want to stay busy and continue telling stories," said.

This includes the story of her parents, Joseph and Bronia Beker, both Holocaust survivors who immigrated to Canada from Poland after the war. Beker spoke passionately about working to publish her parents' memoir, *Joy Runs Deeper*, a project that got her thinking about the idea of legacy. By connecting with her past in this way, Beker hopes she will inspire others to continue telling their own stories in the future. Regarding her own personal legacy, Beker reflected: "I couldn't hope to leave any greater legacy than that of love and kindness. If I've had any hand, through my life's work, in encouraging people to love and celebrate themselves a bit more—and to look at the world in wide-eyed wonder and be less judgemental of one another—I couldn't ask for more."

We spoke a great deal about the importance of storytelling in this context, and particularly about the role it can play in changing how people think about aging adults. By ensuring that aging individuals from all walks of life have a platform from which to tell their stories, we can facilitate productive conversation about the experiences, needs, and desires of this diverse population. In this way, building a better future of aging is less about categorizing challenges into broad themes—like community, healthcare, technology, finances, and identity—and more about asking questions, listening to the answers, and working hard to create real change. By enabling people to live well and on their own terms, we can design positive futures for everyone.

The Future of Aging is thus a call to bring aging adults into the fold—including not only public figures, like Jeanne Beker, but also the millions of other people with a stake in this game. Only by doing this will we overcome the assumptions that have long shaped the engagement (or lack thereof) between the aging population and the world's innovators.

We hope that this book will push industry leaders to build possibilities for an exciting, fulfilling future of aging.

CPSIA information can be obtained
at www.ICGtesting.com
Printed in the USA
LVHW071726250621
691141LV00004B/79

9 780973 081619